Table of Contents

Artists at Work Bulletin Board Title Strip 3

Month	Prep Time	Type of Project	Page
September			
September Bulletin Board			4
Fall Apples	•	construction paper border	5
Classroom Bookworm	•••	toilet roll craft, group activity	6
Getting to Know You	•	human-size drawing	7
Fluorescent Wash	••	fluorescent crayon and tempera painting	8
Fall Trees	•	tissue and construction paper landscape	9
September Scarecrow	••	fabric patchwork	10
October			
October Bulletin Board			12
Tissue Ghosts	••	tissue ghost border	13
Decorative Fall Banner	•••	felt banner, group activity	14
Halloween Lantern	•	construction paper craft	16
Animal Thumbprints	••	stamp pad designs	17
Stand-Up Monster Puppets	••	paper bag construction	18
Marble Design	••	marbles and tempera painting	19
November			
November Bulletin Board			20
Leaf Rubbings	•	leaf and tissue paper border	21
Turkey Wall Decoration	•	paper and leaf group project	22
Edible Turkey	•••	apple and marshmallow craft	23
Woven Paper Place Mats	•	construction paper mats	24
Book Week Bookmark	•	paper bookmarks	26
Fall Leaf Design	•	crayon and watercolor painting	28
December			
December Bulletin Board			29
Noodle Ornaments	••	noodle ornament border	30
Foil Paper Mosaic Mural	••	butcher paper and foil group mural	31
"Hands-On" 3-D Holiday Tree	•	construction paper group craft	32
Ornaments or Decorations	•	construction paper designs	33
Spatter-Painted Holiday Designs	•••	tempera spatter painting	34
Holiday Gift	•••	flour and salt holiday craft	36
January			
January Bulletin Board			37
Paper Doll Snow People	•	construction paper border	38
Patriotic Silhouettes	•	crayon and construction paper silhouettes	40
Winter Wonderland	•	construction paper group bulletin board	42
Snowstorm Paintings	•	tempera and sponge painting	43
Snowflakes	••	coffee filter craft	44
Foil Designs	••	aluminum foil and marker designs	45

February

February Bulletin Board			46
Stencil Heart Designs	•	sponge and tempera border	47
Fuzzy Bear	•	yarn bear	48
Valentine Designs	••	chalk and glue hearts	50
I Can Draw—Part 1	•	pencil cartooning	51
Mr. Lincoln	•	construction paper president	52
George Washington's Hat	•	construction paper hat	54
Yarn Balloon Art	••	balloon, yarn and glue designs	56

March

March Bulletin Board			57
Cartoon Shamrocks	•	construction paper border	58
Blob-Painted Kites	•	tempera painting	59
Jumping O'Jiminy Leprechaun	•	paper craft	60
Starry, Starry Night	•	crayon-resist watercolor painting	62
Patterned Shamrocks	•	crayon or marker designs	63
Fruit and Vegetable Printing	•••	tempera painting, group mural	64

April

April Bulletin Board			65
April Bugs	•	construction paper border	66
Spring Creature	•••	paper towel roll creation	67
Egg Shell Mosaic	•••	mosaic design	68
Teacher's Skirt or Banner	•••	fabric and markers, group activity	69
Bunny Basket	••	milk carton craft	70
Crystallized Egg	••	tempera and salt painting	72

May

May Bulletin Board			73
May Flowers	•	construction paper border	74
Bubble Printing	••	soap bubbles painting	75
Stained Glass Butterflies	•	tissue and construction paper decorations	76
Funny Faces	•••	magazine collage	77
Spring Trees	••	stencil and sponge painting	78
Happy Mother's Day Box	•	construction paper boxes	80

June

June Bulletin Board			82
June Suns	•	construction paper border	83
Macaroni and Bean Collage	•••	dried food collage	84
I Can Draw—Part 2	•	pencil cartooning	85
Happy Father's Day Planter	•••	grass-in-a-cup craft	86
Underwater Scene	••	crayon, tempera and plastic wrap painting	88
June Scene	•	pinhole design	89

Summer

Summer Bulletin Board			90
Summer Sailboats	•	construction paper border	91
Fourth of July Fireworks	•	straw blow painting	92
Summer Sunsets	•	watercolor silhouette designs	93
Felt Hand Puppets	••	sewing with felt	94
Circle Printing	•••	tempera painting activity	96

Bulletin Board Title

Cut out this title strip and use it for a headline on your art bulletin board.

ARTISTS AT WORK

SEPTEMBER BULLETIN BOARD

Have your students make the apples on page 5. Use the apples to make a border on your September bulletin board. The students may need to make several apples each, depending on the size of your bulletin board. As your students complete the arts and crafts projects on pages 6-11, display their work on this board.

ARTISTS AT WORK

September

Arts and Crafts all through the Year IF8561 © MCMLXXXVIII Instructional Fair, Inc.

• CONSTRUCTION PAPER BORDER　　　　　　　　　　　SEPTEMBER

Fall Apples

Materials
9" x 12" red construction paper
9" x 12" green construction paper
apple pattern below
scissors
glue
markers or crayons

Teacher Preparation
1. Use the pattern on this page to draw four apples on a master.
2. Reproduce apples on red construction paper.
3. Use the worm pattern on this page to draw worms on a master.
4. Reproduce worms on green construction paper.

Student Directions
1. Cut out an apple shape. Cut a slit in the apple.
2. Cut out the worm.
3. Using markers or crayons decorate the worm.
4. Accordion fold the worm strip, folding every half inch.
5. Insert the end of the worm strip in the slit in the apple and glue it to the back.
6. Draw and cut out a leaf and stem from green construction paper, then glue these to your apple.

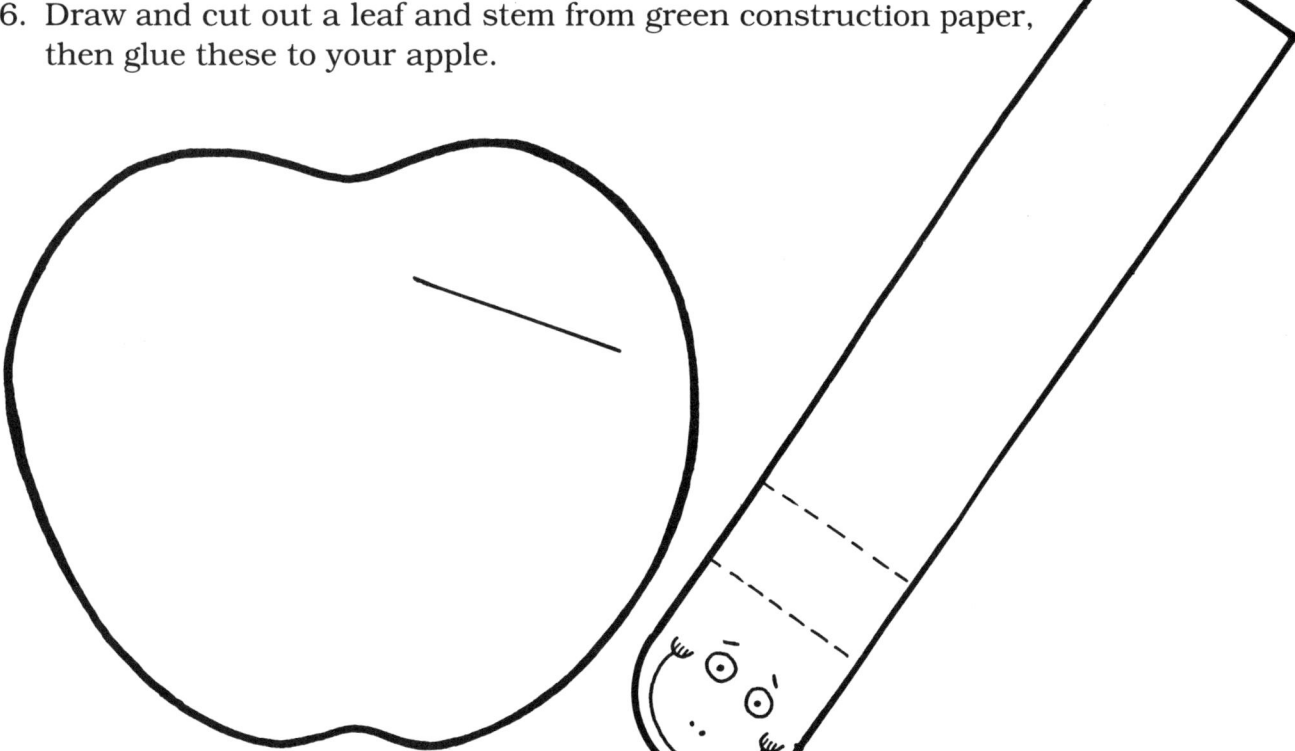

Arts and Crafts all through the Year IF8561　　　　© MCMLXXXVIII Instructional Fair, Inc.

••• TOILET ROLL CRAFT, GROUP ACTIVITY   SEPTEMBER

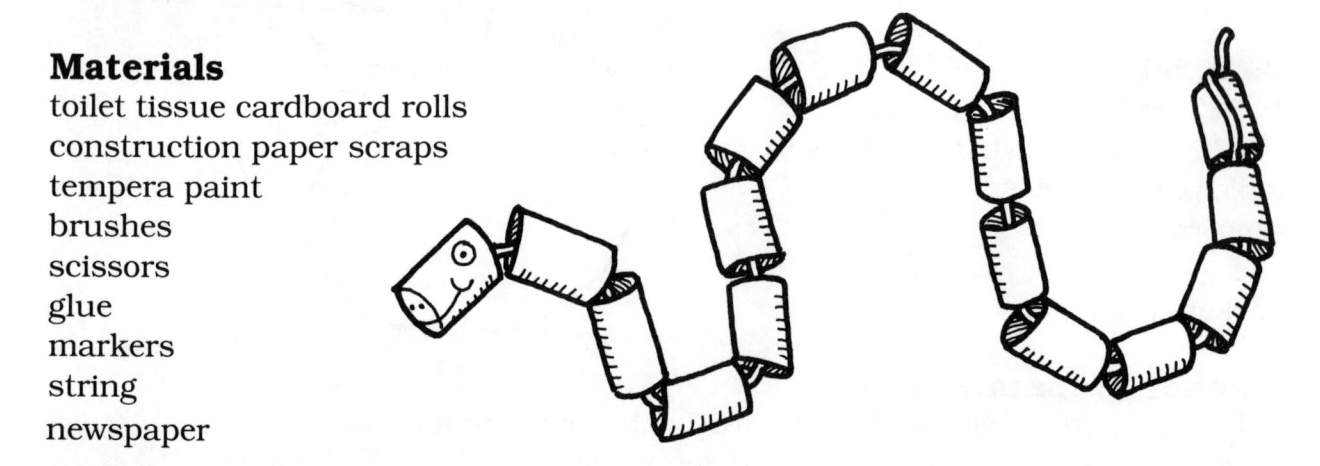

Classroom Bookworm

Materials
toilet tissue cardboard rolls
construction paper scraps
tempera paint
brushes
scissors
glue
markers
string
newspaper

Teacher Preparation
1. Have students bring in toilet tissue rolls.
2. To motivate students, create a bookworm head.
3. Explain that this is going to be the classroom bookworm and that students will be creating the bookworm's body.

Student Directions
1. Think of an interesting design.
2. Paint and decorate a tissue paper roll to form your part of the bookworm's body.

Finishing Touches
When the students have finished decorating their rolls, string all rolls together like a necklace and tie a knot around the last roll. If possible, attach the bookworm along a classroom wall or ledge, or use the bookworm around the art bulletin board or a bulletin board which displays student book reports.

Variation
Instead of making a bookworm, make a dragon for the Chinese New Year.

• HUMAN-SIZE DRAWING　　　　　　　　　　　　　　　　SEPTEMBER

Getting To Know You

Materials
butcher paper
pencils
crayons or markers
masking tape
scissors
tempera paint (optional)
brushes (if paint is used)
newspaper (if paint is used)

Teacher Preparation
1. Cut one sheet of butcher paper per student, sized to the student's height.
2. Prepare an area where students can work on the floor.
3. Have students work in teams of two or three, depending on available space.

Student Directions
1. Tape the butcher paper to the floor.
2. Lie down on the floor on top of your butcher paper.
3. Have your partner draw an outline of you with a crayon.
4. Do the same for your partner on another piece of butcher paper.
5. Using crayons, markers, or paints, draw and color your face and clothes inside your shape.

Note
Two figures can be cut out, stapled or glued together and stuffed with crumpled newspaper. These figures can be displayed around the room. They are especially fun for Back-to-School Night.

Arts and Crafts all through the Year IF8561　　　　© MCMLXXXVIII Instructional Fair, Inc.

•• FLUORESCENT CRAYON AND TEMPERA PAINTING   SEPTEMBER

Fluorescent Wash

Materials
landscape pictures
white drawing paper,
 one sheet per student
fluorescent crayons
black tempera paint
brushes
pencils
newspaper

Teacher Preparation
1. Dilute black paint to a watery consistency.
2. Show students landscape pictures and discuss possibilities for drawings.

Student Directions
1. Cover your desk with newspaper.
2. Look at the pictures for ideas for your drawing.
3. Draw a picture lightly with a pencil.
4. Color your picture with crayons. Press hard. For best results, use a variety of colors.
5. Brush your entire picture with diluted black tempera paint. The fluorescent colors will show brightly through the black paint.

• TISSUE AND CONSTRUCTION PAPER LANDSCAPE — SEPTEMBER

Fall Trees

Materials
light blue construction paper, one sheet per student
brown construction paper
tissue paper, fall leaf colors
crayons
glue
pencils with erasers

Teacher Preparation
1. Cut tissue paper into 1" squares.
2. Take your students on a walking trip around the school grounds to observe sizes, shapes and colors of fall trees.

Student Directions
1. Using brown construction paper, tear one or more tree trunk shapes. Glue your tree trunks to the light blue construction paper. To make your design more interesting, tear tree limb shapes and add them to your trees. Draw and color in the ground around the trees.
2. Use tissue paper squares to make the foliage. Wrap each square around a pencil eraser, dip it in glue and apply it to your tree. Add different color leaves to your trees until they are as full as you like.

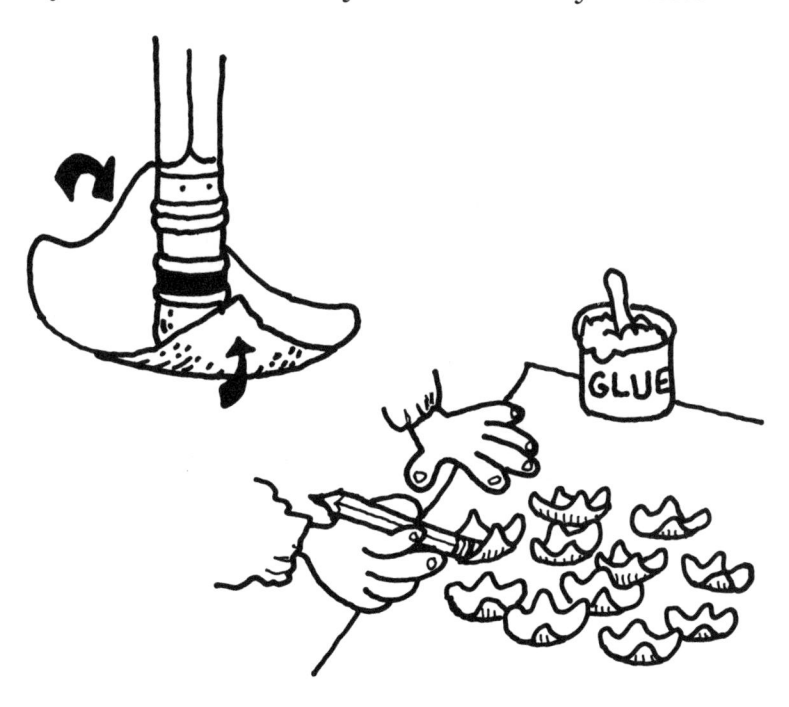

•• FABRIC PATCHWORK   SEPTEMBER

September Scarecrow

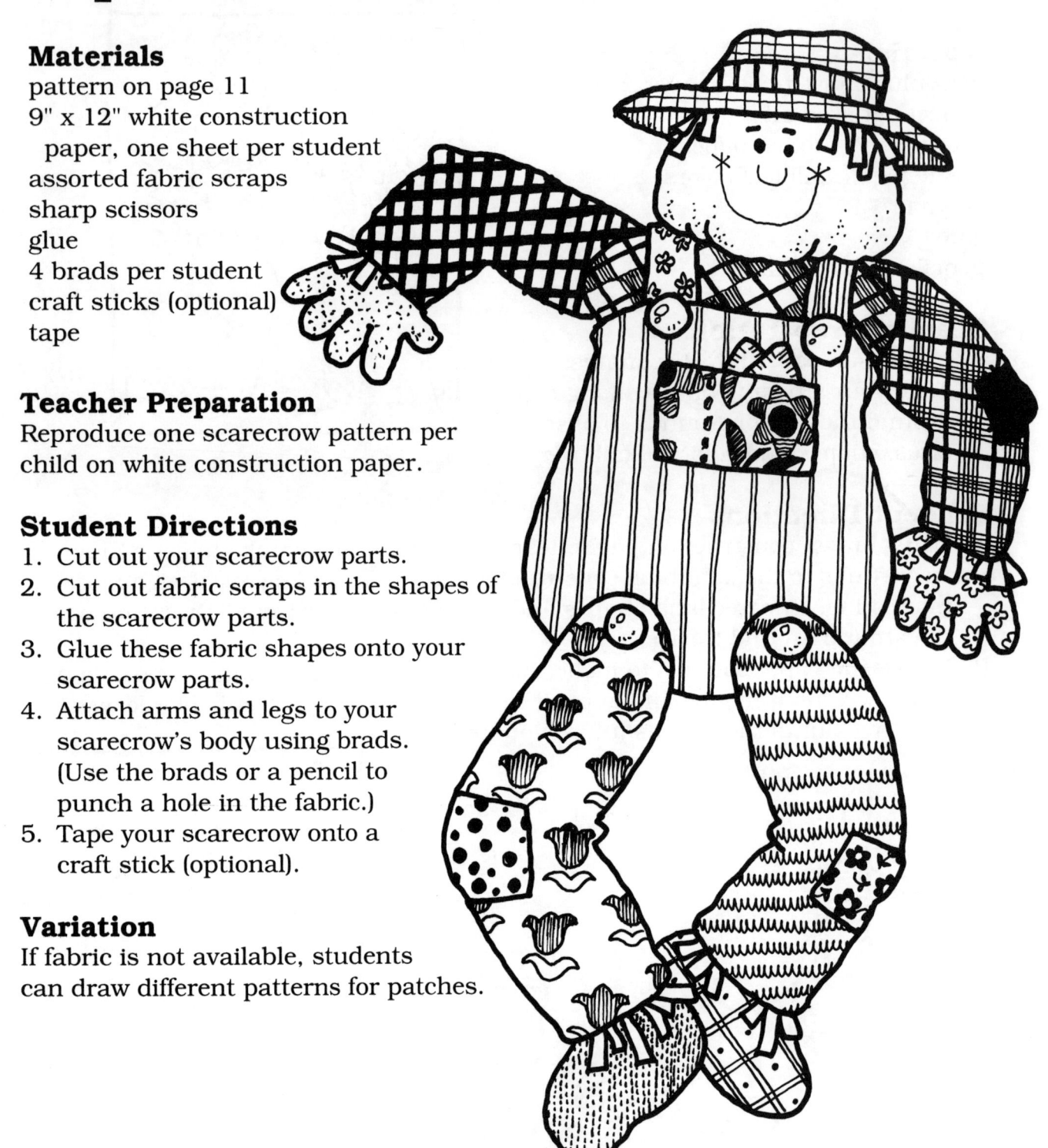

Materials
pattern on page 11
9" x 12" white construction
  paper, one sheet per student
assorted fabric scraps
sharp scissors
glue
4 brads per student
craft sticks (optional)
tape

Teacher Preparation
Reproduce one scarecrow pattern per child on white construction paper.

Student Directions
1. Cut out your scarecrow parts.
2. Cut out fabric scraps in the shapes of the scarecrow parts.
3. Glue these fabric shapes onto your scarecrow parts.
4. Attach arms and legs to your scarecrow's body using brads. (Use the brads or a pencil to punch a hole in the fabric.)
5. Tape your scarecrow onto a craft stick (optional).

Variation
If fabric is not available, students can draw different patterns for patches.

Arts and Crafts all through the Year IF8561   10   © MCMLXXXVIII Instructional Fair, Inc.

•• FABRIC PATCHWORK　　　　　　　　　　　　　　　　　　SEPTEMBER

September Scarecrow Pattern

Arts and Crafts all through the Year IF8561　　　11　　　© MCMLXXXVIII Instructional Fair, Inc.

OCTOBER BULLETIN BOARD

Have your students make the ghosts on page 13. Use the ghosts to make borders on your October bulletin board. The students may need to make several ghosts each, depending on the size of your bulletin board. As your students complete the arts and crafts projects on pages 14-19, display their work on this board.

ARTISTS AT WORK

October

Arts and Crafts all through the Year IF8561 © MCMLXXXVIII Instructional Fair, Inc.

•• TISSUE GHOST BORDER OCTOBER

Tissue Ghosts

Materials
aluminum foil
white tissues
yarn (preferably orange or black)
orange and black markers
lollipops (optional)

Teacher Preparation
1. Ask your students to save aluminum foil from their lunches or bring small pieces from home.
2. Cut yarn into 6" pieces, one piece per student.

Student Directions
1. Squeeze your aluminum foil into a small ball.
2. Lay two tissues, one on top of the other, as shown.
3. Put your aluminum foil ball in the center of the tissue, then tie a piece of yarn around the tissue and ball to form your ghost's head.
4. Carefully draw a scary ghost face using a marker.

Variation
If you wish to give your students a treat, form the ghost around a lollipop instead of an aluminum foil ball.

Arts and Crafts all through the Year IF8561 © MCMLXXXVIII Instructional Fair, Inc.

••• FELT BANNER, GROUP ACTIVITY   OCTOBER

Decorative Fall Banner

Materials
fruit patterns on page 15
large piece of brown felt or corduroy, approximately 2' x 3'
felt in fruit colors
piece of fabric for bowl
oaktag
glue
scissors
orange cotton fringe (optional)
2'4" piece of wood doweling
various colors of yarn (optional)

Teacher Preparation
1. Fold back the top edge of the felt or corduroy banner. Then either stitch or glue down the edge, leaving an opening for the doweling.
2. Enlarge the fruit pattern pieces to desired size. Make fruit tracers out of oaktag.
3. Cut felt into pieces slightly larger than the patterns.
4. Assign partners. Each set of partners will make one fruit shape.
5. Draw a large bowl on fabric. Assign one or two students to cut out the bowl and glue it to the banner.

Student Directions
1. Work in teams of two. One of you traces a fruit pattern onto felt and one of you cuts out the fruit shape.
2. Glue your felt shape to the banner in an appropriate place.
3. Outline each fruit piece with a corresponding color of yarn (optional).

Finishing Touches
Some students may choose to work on a decorative border using leftover felt scraps and yarn.

Help your students fold under the bottom of the banner and stitch or glue it down as you would a hem. Glue or loosely stitch fringe to the bottom of the banner.

Note
This bright banner will cheer up your classrooom on Back-to-School Night.

Arts and Crafts all through the Year IF8561   © MCMLXXXVIII Instructional Fair, Inc.

••• FELT BANNER, GROUP ACTIVITY   OCTOBER

Decorative Fall Banner Patterns

Arts and Crafts all through the Year IF8561

• CONSTRUCTION PAPER CRAFT   OCTOBER

Halloween Lantern

Materials
9" x 12" orange construction paper,
  one sheet per student
black construction paper scraps
scissors
glue
tape
string
orange and black crepe paper streamers (optional)

Student Directions
1. Fold orange construction paper in half.
2. With a ruler, mark lines every 1" as shown. Leave 2" at the top.
3. Cut on the lines you have drawn.
4. Unfold the paper and tape the ends of the lantern together.
5. Cut out eyes, nose and mouth from black construction paper, then glue them to your lantern.
6. Glue on crepe paper tails.
7. In order to hang your lantern, poke holes and thread with a string as shown.

Variation
Use a black lantern to make a cat. Use orange for eyes, nose, mouth and whiskers.

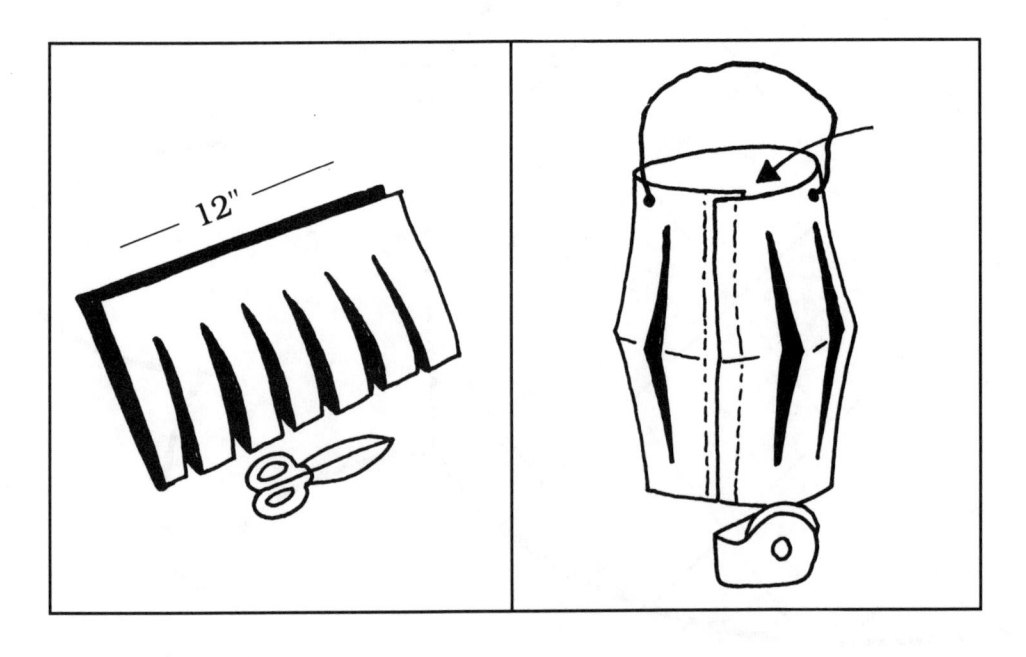

•• STAMP PAD DESIGNS   OCTOBER

Animal Thumbprints

Materials
several stamp pads (black or purple)
any white paper
crayons and markers

Teacher Preparation
1. Cut white paper to approximately 4 1/4" x 5 1/2"; cut several sheets per student.
2. Demonstrate to students how to make thumbprint animals.
3. Remind your students they can use any finger or thumb.

Student Directions
1. Roll your fingertip or thumb over the stamp pad.
2. Press it onto your white paper.
3. With crayons or markers, add animal details (eyes, nose, whiskers, teeth, etc.).
4. See how many different animals you can create.

Finishing Touches
Several sheets can be stapled at the top to form a notepad.

Variations
This activity can be used to make greeting cards, stories, book covers or wrapping paper.

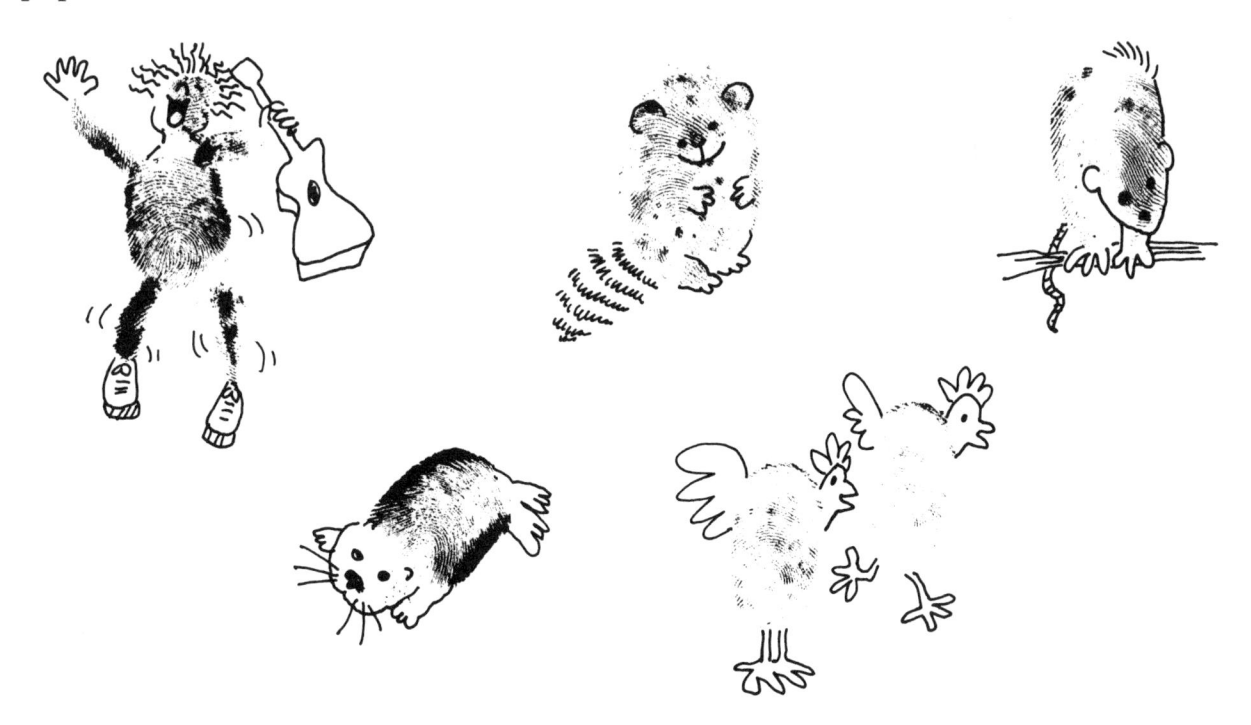

Arts and Crafts all through the Year IF8561   © MCMLXXXVIII Instructional Fair, Inc.

•• PAPER BAG CONSTRUCTION   OCTOBER

Stand-Up Monster Puppets

Materials
2 brown lunch bags per student
newspaper
string or yarn
fabric scraps
tissue paper scraps
construction paper scraps, all sizes
buttons, rickrack and other easy-to-find
  decorative items
markers
scissors
glue
tape

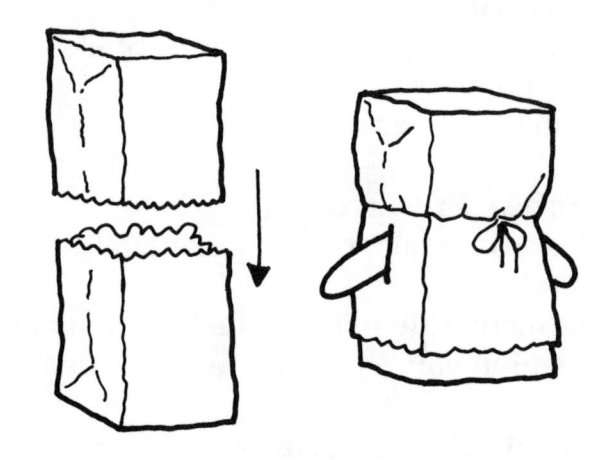

Student Directions
1. Fill two lunch bags with loosely crumpled newspaper.
2. Fit one of the bags over the other, and tie it loosely one third of the way down using string or yarn as shown.
3. Use materials from the art table to create faces, hair, clothes, and even arms and feet for your monster puppets.

Arts and Crafts all through the Year IF8561   © MCMLXXXVIII Instructional Fair, Inc.

•• MARBLES AND TEMPERA PAINTING   OCTOBER

Marble Design

Materials
12" x 18" construction paper
shallow boxes, about the same size
   as the paper
tempera paint, various colors
small jars
marbles
plastic spoons
newspaper

Teacher Preparation
1. Cover the art center table with newspaper.
2. Set up materials at the art center.
3. Pour the paint into jars.
4. Put several marbles into each jar.

Student Directions
1. Place construction paper in the bottom of your box.
2. Remove a marble from the jar using a spoon.
3. Place your marble in the box.
4. Roll the marble around to make a design.
5. Take out the marble and place it back into the jar.
6. Repeat the process with other colors.

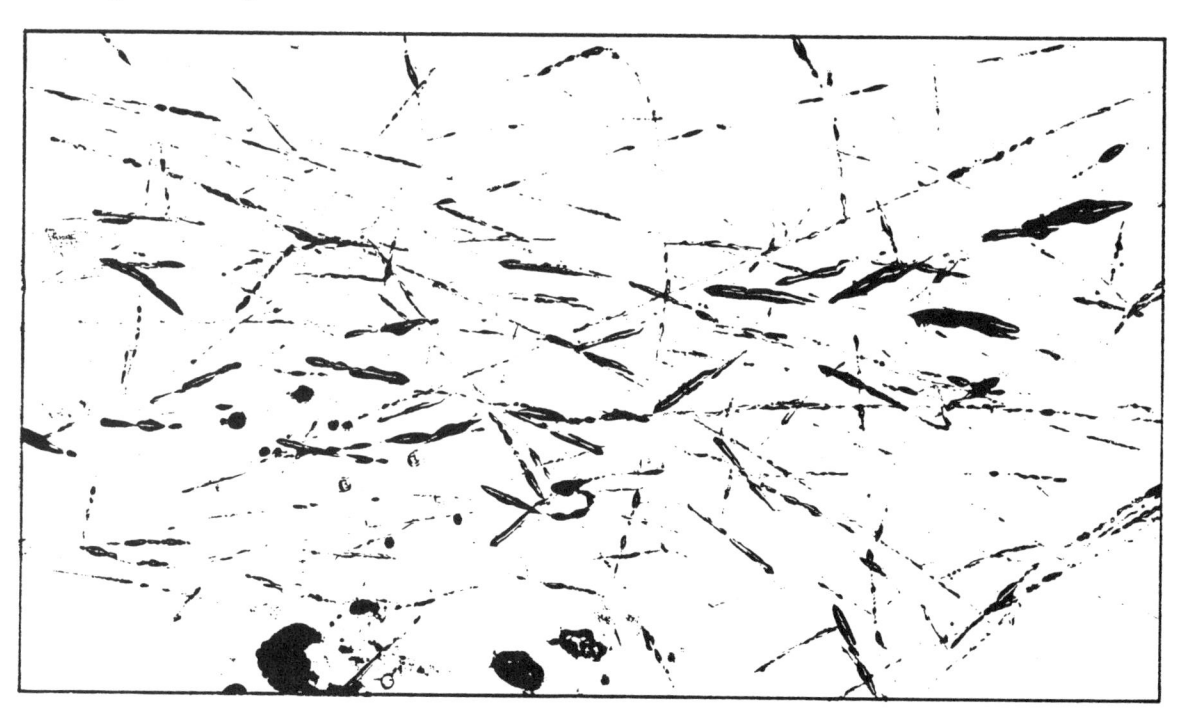

Arts and Crafts all through the Year IF8561   © MCMLXXXVIII Instructional Fair, Inc.

NOVEMBER BULLETIN BOARD

Have your students make the leaf rubbings on page 21. Use the rubbings to make borders on your November bulletin board. The students may need to make several rubbings each, depending on the size of your bulletin board. As your students complete the arts and crafts projects on pages 22-28, display their work on this board.

ARTISTS AT WORK

November

Arts and Crafts all through the Year IF8561 © MCMLXXXVIII Instructional Fair, Inc.

• LEAF AND TISSUE PAPER BORDER   NOVEMBER

Leaf Rubbings

Materials
tissue paper in fall colors
white construction paper
fresh leaves
broken pieces of brown crayon
liquid starch (watered down white glue
  or polymer gel can also be used)
paint brushes
brown markers
newspaper
scissors

Teacher Preparation
1. Cut tissue paper and construction paper into 5" squares.
2. Take the class on a walking trip around the school grounds to find fresh leaves, or have students bring leaves from home. Have students collect as many varied and interestingly veined leaves as possible.

Student Directions
1. Cover your desk with newspaper.
2. Place a leaf on the table with the vein side up.
3. Put a 5" square of tissue paper over the leaf and rub gently with the side of a crayon until a leaf vein pattern appears.
4. Trace the shape of the leaf with a marker. Cut out the leaf shape.
5. Take a white construction paper square and brush it with liquid starch. Then place the tissue paper with the leaf print on top of the construction paper, and brush the paper again with liquid starch. Let the rubbing dry.
6. Cut out the leaf shape (optional).

• PAPER AND LEAF GROUP PROJECT   NOVEMBER

Turkey Wall Decoration

Materials
brown or orange butcher paper
scissors
glue
colorful fall leaves

Teacher Preparation
1. Take your class on a short walking trip around the school grounds and have students collect a variety of colorful fall leaves. Leaves should not be too dry.
2. Using a large sheet of brown or orange butcher paper, sketch a large turkey shape as shown. Assign students to cut out the turkey shape.
3. Staple the turkey shape to the bulletin board.

Student Directions
Take turns gluing or stapling on leaves to form the tail feathers of the turkey.

Variation
Instead of using leaves, have the students trace their own hand shapes on construction paper, cut them out, and glue them to the turkey body. Add the bulletin board title: "We Are Thankful For Our Hands." Students can write short phrases about things they do with their hands for which they are thankful, such as writing letters, waving to friends or making cookies. Staple the students' phrases to the bulletin board around the turkey.

••• APPLE AND MARSHMALLOW CRAFT　　　　　　　　　NOVEMBER

Edible Turkey

Materials
apples, one per student
large marshmallows, one per student
small colored marshmallows or gum drops
cloves or raisins, two per student
curled carrot strips, several per student (optional)
toothpicks

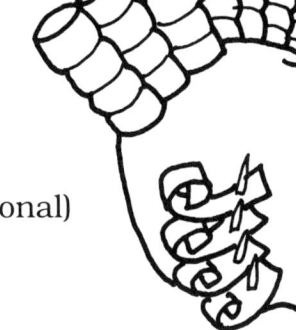

Teacher Preparation
Bring in the above foods or ask
your students to bring them in.

Student Activity
1. Attach the turkey head (large marshmallow) to the body (apple) with a toothpick.
2. Attach eyes (two cloves or two raisins) to the head with toothpicks.
3. Attach tail feathers (small marshmallows or gum drops) to the body with toothpicks.
4. Attach the side wings (curled carrot strips) to body with toothpicks.

Arts and Crafts all through the Year IF8561　　　© MCMLXXXVIII Instructional Fair, Inc.

• CONSTRUCTION PAPER MATS NOVEMBER

Woven Paper Place Mats

Materials
Thanksgiving patterns on page 25
12" x 18" construction paper in fall colors,
 two different colored sheets per student
9" x 12" white construction paper,
 one sheet per student
crayons
scissors
glue

Teacher Preparation
Reproduce Thanksgiving patterns
on construction paper.

Student Directions
1. Take one piece of construction paper and draw a line one inch from the top. Fold the construction paper in half as shown.
2. Draw curvy lines about 1 1/2" apart from the top line to the fold as shown.
3. Cut the lines from the bottom up, from the fold to the line.
4. Take the second piece of construction paper and cut 1 1/2" strips crosswise as shown.
5. Use these strips to weave through the strips of the first sheet of construction paper.
6. When you have finished weaving, glue the ends of the strips down on the back side and trim the edges of your place mat.
7. Color and cut out Thanksgiving patterns and glue them to your place mat. Use your mat to decorate your family's Thanksgiving table.

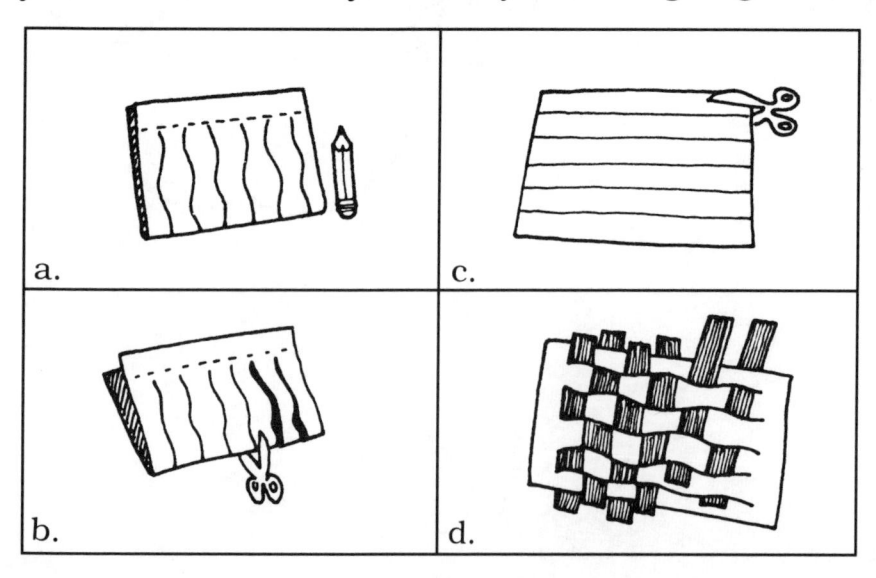

Arts and Crafts all through the Year IF8561   © MCMLXXXVIII Instructional Fair, Inc.

• CONSTRUCTION PAPER MATSNOVEMBER

Woven Paper Place Mat Patterns

• PAPER BOOKMARKS   NOVEMBER

Book Week Bookmark

Materials
animal patterns on pages 26-27
9" x 12" white construction paper
scissors
glue
yarn
decorative items such as sequins, yarn, rick-rack, buttons, etc.

Teacher Preparation
Reproduce one pattern per student on construction paper.

Student Directions
1. Cut out the animal pattern of your choice.
2. Decorate your animal by adding eyes, ears, whiskers, nose, etc.
3. Glue strands of yarn for tail.

Note
National Children's Book Week is in November.

- PAPER BOOKMARKS   NOVEMBER

Book Week Bookmark Patterns

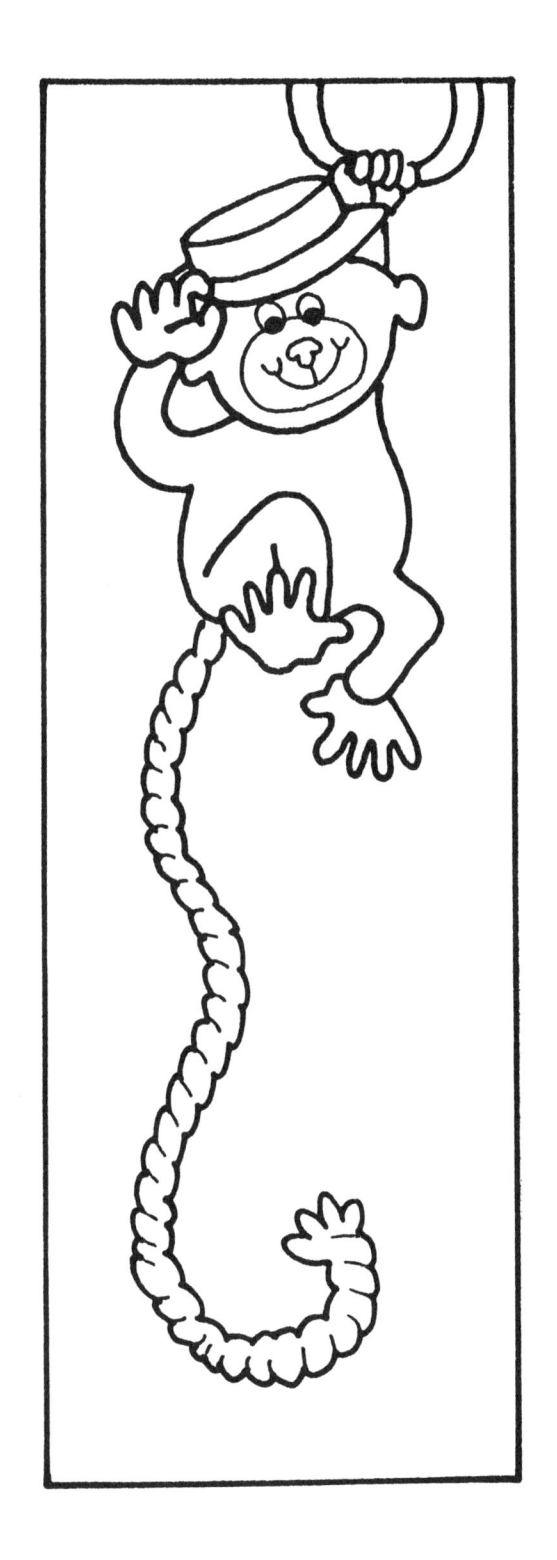

• CRAYON AND WATERCOLOR PAINTING   NOVEMBER

Fall Leaf Design

Materials
9" x 12" white construction paper, one sheet per student
fresh leaves, various shapes and sizes
watercolor paints in fall leaf colors
brushes
black crayons

Teacher Preparation
Take your class on a walking trip around the school grounds and have the students collect leaves of various shapes and sizes.

Student Directions
1. One by one, gently trace the outlines of a variety of leaves onto white construction paper. Make sure to fill the entire page. Trace over each leaf shape with a thick line of black crayon.
2. Paint the inside of each leaf shape with different fall colors of watercolor paint. The black crayon outline will keep the colors from running together.

DECEMBER BULLETIN BOARD

Have your students make the noodle ornaments on page 30. Use the ornaments to make borders on your December bulletin board. The students may need to make several ornaments each, depending on the size of your bulletin board. As your students complete the arts and crafts projects on pages 31-36, display their work on this board.

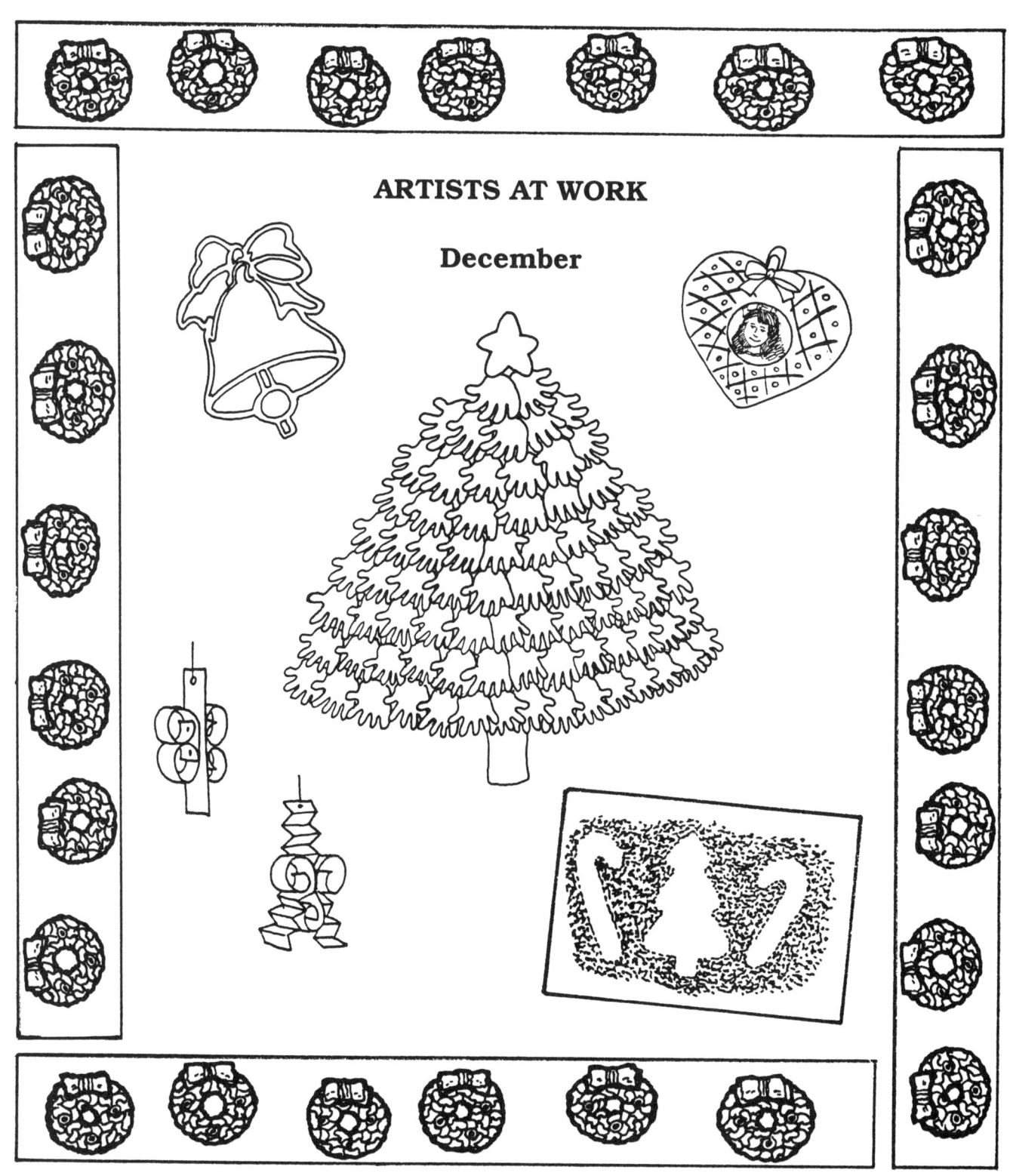

ARTISTS AT WORK

December

Arts and Crafts all through the Year IF8561   © MCMLXXXVIII Instructional Fair, Inc.

•• NOODLE ORNAMENT BORDER DECEMBER

Noodle Ornaments

Materials
noodles of all shapes
construction paper in holiday colors
white glue
toothpicks

Teacher Preparation
Cut construction paper into 3" circles.

Student Directions
1. Using different noodles, make an attractive arrangement on your round piece of construction paper.
2. Using a toothpick, glue each piece onto your circle.
3. Let dry.

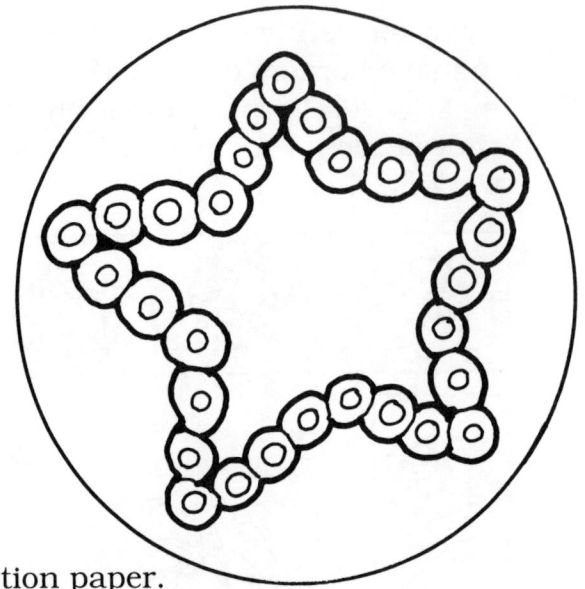

•• BUTCHER PAPER AND FOIL GROUP MURAL   DECEMBER

Foil Paper Mosaic Mural

Materials
butcher paper at least 3' x 4' (the larger the size, the more stunning the result)
various colors of foil-type wrapping paper
scissors
glue
pencils
thick black markers

Teacher Preparation
Staple up butcher paper to fit the bulletin board or wall area.

Student Directions
1. Using a pencil, help your teacher draw large, simple Christmas or Hanukkah designs on the butcher paper.
2. Outline the designs with a thick black marker.
3. Tear or cut small pieces of foil paper to fit into the different parts of the mosaic.

Arts and Crafts all through the Year IF8561

• CONSTRUCTION PAPER GROUP CRAFT   DECEMBER

"Hands-On" 3-D Holiday Tree

Materials
green construction paper
scissors
pencils
glue or stapler

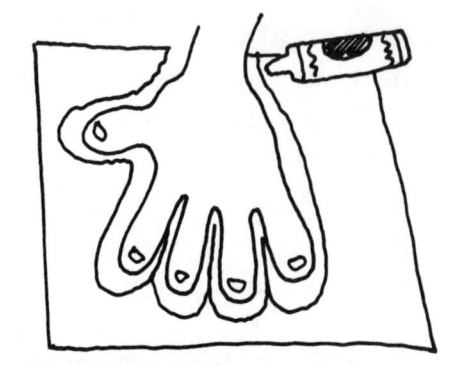

Teacher Preparation
Cut green construction paper into 6" squares.

Student Directions
1. Trace your hand onto the green paper, then cut out the hand shape.
2. Write a Christmas message or wish on your hand shape.
3. "Curl" each finger of the hand shape by wrapping the fingers around a pencil, one at a time.

Finishing Touches
Collect all of your students' "hands" and attach them to the bulletin board in a triangular tree shape. Students can make paper chains and construction paper ornaments to decorate the tree.

• CONSTRUCTION PAPER DESIGNS   DECEMBER

Ornaments or Package Decorations

Materials
construction paper, red and green for Christmas, blue and white for Hanukkah
stapler
glue or tape
string

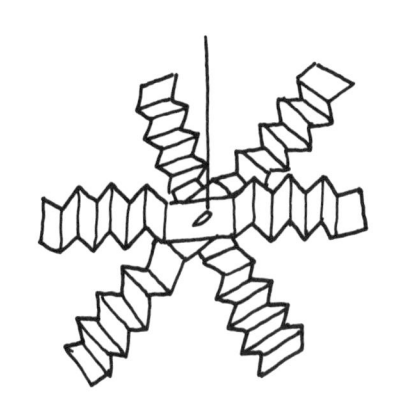

Teacher Preparation
1. Cut construction paper into 1" x 9" strips: six paper strips to each student, three of each color.
2. After the students have arranged the strips in alternate colors, help them staple the strips together in the middle as shown.

Student Directions
1. Create various designs by folding and gluing or curling the top and bottom ends of the stapled strips as shown.
2. Hang the ornaments with string or tape them to holiday packages.

Note
There are endless ways to fold the paper strips. Encourage students to use their imaginations.

Ways to Staple

Ways to Fold

Arts and Crafts all through the Year IF8561   33   © MCMLXXXVIII Instructional Fair, Inc.

••• TEMPERA SPATTER PAINTING   DECEMBER

Spatter-Painted Holiday Designs

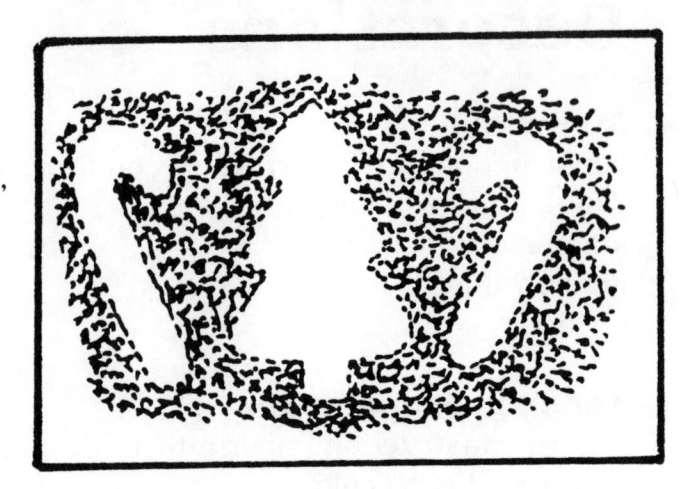

Materials
holiday shapes patterns on page 35
oaktag
various dark colors of construction paper,
    one sheet per student
construction paper for frames,
    one sheet per student
white tempera paint
old toothbrushes
craft sticks (ice cream sticks)
aluminum pie plates
pins
newspaper

Teacher Preparation
1. Duplicate one page of holiday shapes per student on oaktag.
2. Pour small amounts of white paint into pie plates for students to share.

Student Directions
1. Cover your desk with newspaper.
2. Cut out the holiday shapes you want for your painting.
3. Pin the shapes in a design you like onto a piece of construction paper.
4. Dip a toothbrush in the paint and hold it over your design.
5. Rub the craft stick over the toothbrush rubbing away from your face.
   Paint will spatter in tiny drops on your design. Let your painting dry.
6. Remove the pins and shapes. Frame your painting.

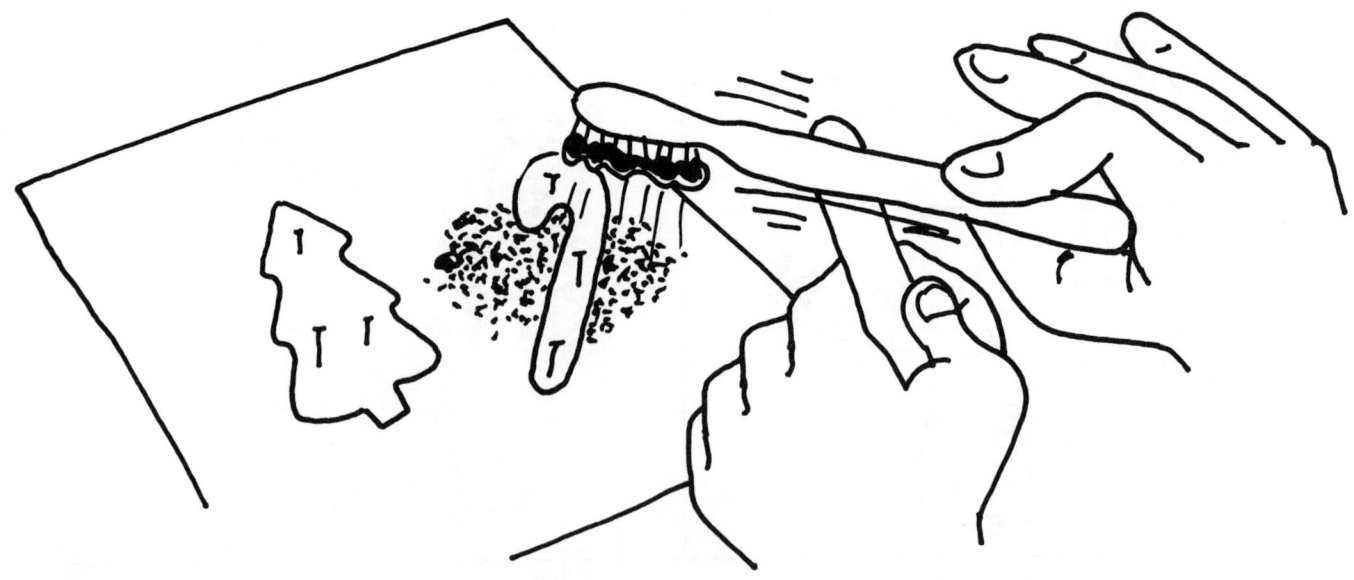

Arts and Crafts all through the Year IF8561   34   © MCMLXXXVIII Instructional Fair, Inc.

••• TEMPERA SPATTER PAINTING   DECEMBER

Spatter-Painted Holiday Design Patterns

Arts and Crafts all through the Year IF8561   © MCMLXXXVIII Instructional Fair, Inc.

••• FLOUR AND SALT HOLIDAY CRAFT DECEMBER

Holiday Gift

Materials
2 cups flour
1 cup salt
2/3 cups water
felt tipped pens
cookie cutter in shape of heart
  or simple holiday shape
paper clips, one per student
individual photographs of students
donut cutter or round cutting tool smaller
  in diameter than the photographs
rolling pin (optional)
clear plastic spray, available in art supply
  stores (optional)

Teacher Preparation
1. The night before make the following recipe: Mix dry ingredients with hands and then add water. Depending on the amount of moisture in the air, more water may be needed. You should end up with a mixture the consistency of stiff pie dough.
2. Roll out dough with a rolling pin, or pat dough out to about 1/4" thick.
3. During class or the night before, cut out dough with cookie cutter. Using donut cutter or round cutting tool, cut a hole in the center of each shape.

Student Directions
1. Cut out a shape from the dough with a cookie cutter.
2. With the donut cutter, cut a hole in the center of your shape.
3. Push a paper clip through the top of the shape to serve as a hanger.
4. Carve your initials in the back of the shape.
5. Air dry your shape for several days.
6. When your shape is dry, decorate it with felt tipped pens.
7. Have your teacher help you spray the shape with clear plastic (optional).
8. Carefully place glue around the edges of the hole on the back of the shape.
9. Glue your photograph on the back of the shape. If the hole is larger than the photograph, glue your picture onto a piece of round construction paper, then glue the construction paper to back of the shape.
10. Tie a ribbon around the paper clip.

Arts and Crafts all through the Year IF8561

JANUARY BULLETIN BOARD

Have your students make the snow people on pages 38-39. Use the snow people to make borders on your January bulletin board. The students may need to make several chains of snow people each, depending on the size of your bulletin board. As your students complete the arts and crafts projects on pages 40-45, display their work on this board.

ARTISTS AT WORK

January

Arts and Crafts all through the Year IF8561 © MCMLXXXVIII Instructional Fair, Inc.

• CONSTRUCTION PAPER BORDER   JANUARY

Paper Doll Snow People

Materials
patterns on page 39
white ditto paper, one sheet per student
scraps of colored construction paper
scissors
markers
glue

Teacher Preparation
Reproduce snow people patterns on ditto paper.

Student Directions
1. Cut outside rectangle along solid line.
2. Make an accordion fold with snow person showing on top.
3. Cut out your snow person. (Do not cut off the entire fold.)
4. Draw clothes and features.
5. Cut out hat shapes from colored construction paper and glue hats on the snow people.

Arts and Crafts all through the Year IF8561   © MCMLXXXVIII Instructional Fair, Inc.

• CONSTRUCTION PAPER BORDER　　　　　　　　　　　　　　　　　　　JANUARY

Paper Doll Snow People

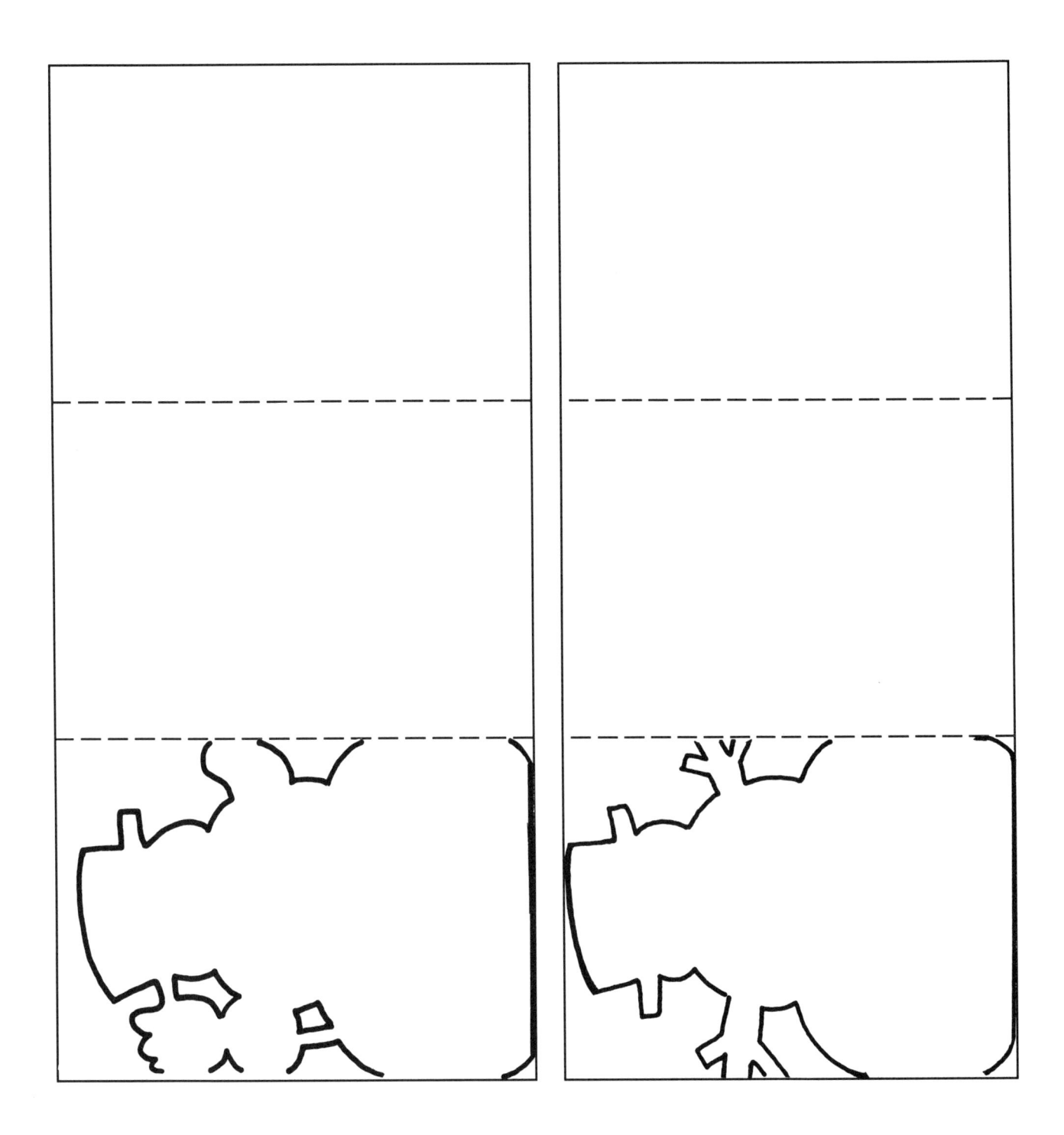

Arts and Crafts all through the Year IF8561　　　　© MCMLXXXVIII Instructional Fair, Inc.

• CRAYON AND CONSTRUCTION PAPER SILHOUETTES   JANUARY

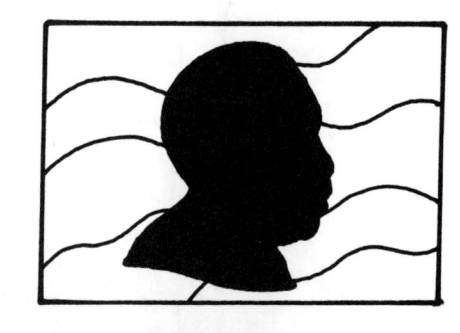

Patriotic Silhouettes

Materials
Martin Luther King, Lincoln and Washington silhouettes on page 41
9" x 12" white construction paper, two sheets per student
black construction paper
red and blue crayons
scissors
glue

Teacher Preparation
1. Reproduce silhouettes on white construction paper, one silhouette per student.
2. Use examples below to help students create their own crayon design.

Student Directions
1. Cut out the silhouette pattern and trace it on black construction paper. Then cut out your black silhouette.
2. Use red and blue crayons on white construction paper to create a background design. Fill your entire paper with the design.
3. Glue your silhouette of Martin Luther King, Lincoln, or Washington to your red, white and blue background design.

Note
This activity can also be used in February for President's Day.

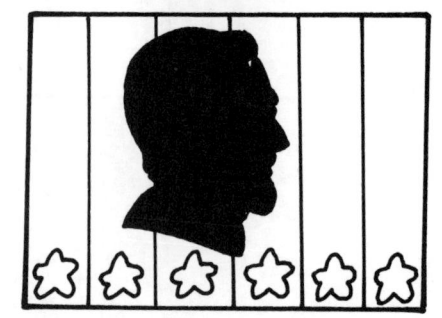

Arts and Crafts all through the Year IF8561   © MCMLXXXVIII Instructional Fair, Inc.

• CRAYON AND CONSTRUCTION PAPER SILHOUETTES   JANUARY

Patriotic Silhouette Patterns

Arts and Crafts all through the Year IF8561   41   © MCMLXXXVIII Instructional Fair, Inc.

• CONSTRUCTION PAPER GROUP BULLETIN BOARD   JANUARY

Winter Wonderland

Materials
large sheet of dark blue or black butcher paper (bulletin board size)
white butcher paper, 2'-3' per child
white construction paper for ground
colored construction paper
holiday wrapping paper (optional)
glue
scissors
crayons or markers
pencils

Teacher Preparation
1. Cover a large bulletin board with dark butcher paper.
2. Cut out white butcher paper for the ground and staple it to the bottom of the bulletin board.

Student Directions
1. Lightly sketch a large snow person shape on your white butcher paper with a pencil. When you are satisfied with your shape, trace its outline with a marker.
2. Cut out your shape.
3. Decorate your snow person with a hat, scarf, mittens, etc., using colored construction paper and wrapping paper.
4. Add details with markers or crayons.

Finishing Touches
Arrange the finished snow people on the bulletin board. Students can add trees, snowflakes and various snow-capped buildings to complete the background.

Arts and Crafts all through the Year IF8561   © MCMLXXXVIII Instructional Fair, Inc.

• TEMPERA AND SPONGE PAINTING JANUARY

Snowstorm Paintings

Materials
dark blue or black construction paper, one sheet per student
construction paper, all colors and sizes
thick white tempera paint
small pieces of sponge
tin pie plates
aluminum foil
glue
scissors

Teacher Preparation
Cut colored construction paper into various sizes of triangular, square and rectangular shapes.

Student Directions
1. Choose a variety of construction paper shapes, and use them to create a nighttime city scene of buildings and houses on black or dark blue construction paper.
2. When you are satisfied with your scene, glue the paper shapes in place.
3. Cut window shapes from aluminum foil and glue them to the buildings.
4. Pour a small amount of white tempera paint into a tin pie plate. Dip a sponge piece into the paint, then blot the paint gently onto the paper above your buildings to create a snowstorm effect.

Arts and Crafts all through the Year IF8561 © MCMLXXXVIII Instructional Fair, Inc.

•• COFFEE FILTER CRAFT　　　　　　　　　　　　JANUARY

Snowflakes

Materials
coffee filters (Mr. Coffee type), one per student
scissors
watercolors
brushes
water containers
newspaper

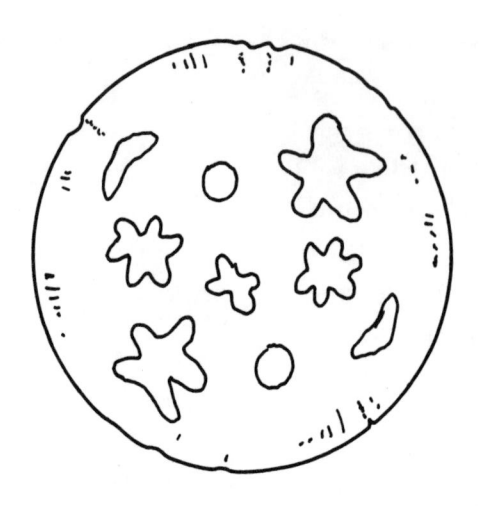

Student Directions
1. Cover your desk with newspaper.
2. First, fold your coffee filter in half, then fold it into thirds.
3. Cut out patterns on the edges. Be careful not to cut off the entire edge.
4. Open the filter and paint it.

Variations
1. Instead of painting the coffee filter, leave the filter folded and dip the edges into watercolors.
2. Repeat in February, with heart shapes cut from the filter.

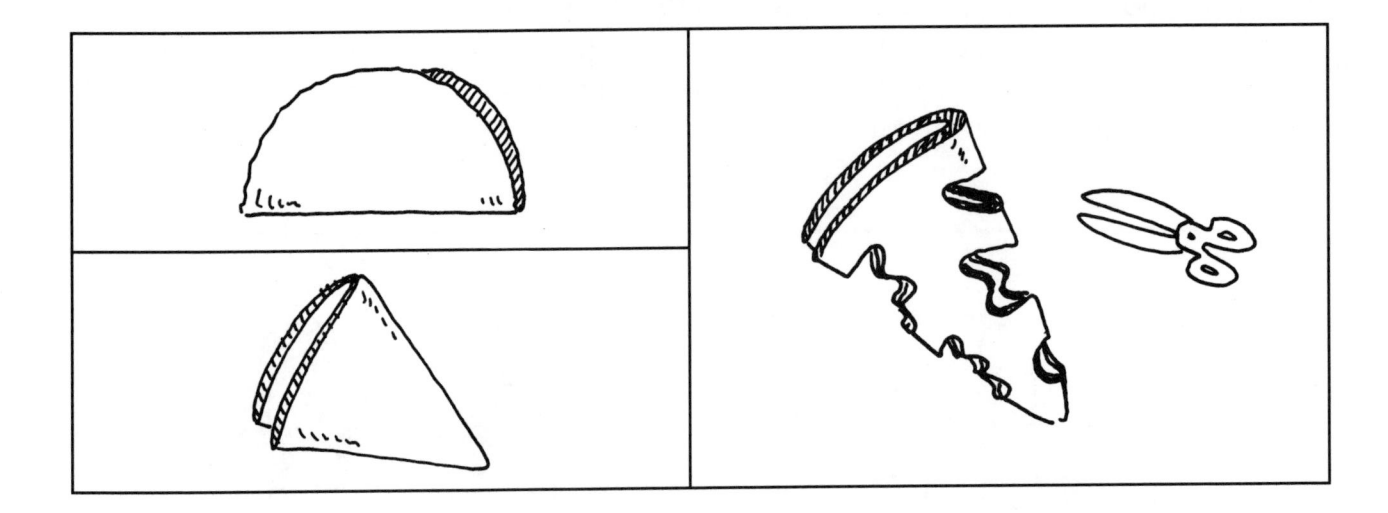

Arts and Crafts all through the Year IF8561　　　　© MCMLXXXVIII Instructional Fair, Inc.

•• ALUMINUM FOIL AND MARKER DESIGNS   JANUARY

Foil Designs

Materials
tagboard
aluminum foil
white glue
tape
yarn
permanent felt tipped marking pens
 in assorted colors (water-based
 markers will not work)

Teacher Preparation
Cut tagboard into approximately 10" squares, one per student.

Student Directions
1. Draw an abstract design with glue on your tagboard square.
2. Lay yarn on top of your glue design.
3. Cover the entire square with aluminum foil. Fold the extra foil around the edges and tape it down on the back.
4. Press down the foil so the yarn stands out.
5. Using permanent markers, color each section of your design a different color.
6. Use black to color the outline of the yarn.

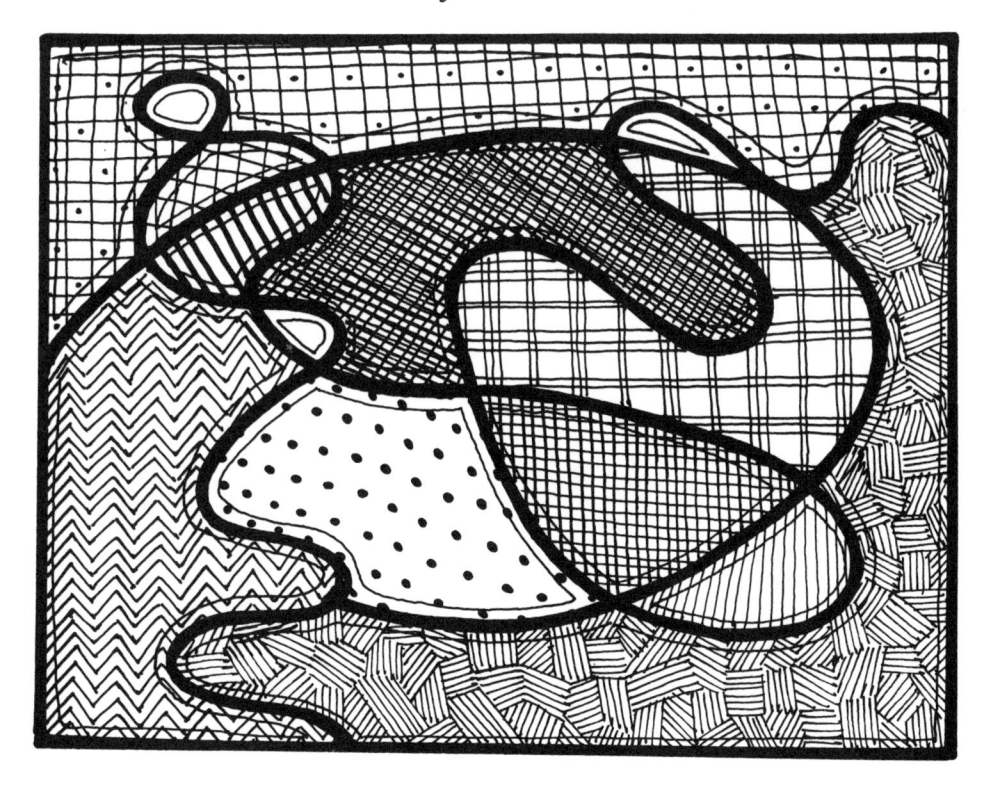

Arts and Crafts all through the Year IF8561

FEBRUARY BULLETIN BOARD

Have your students make the heart strips on page 47. Use the strips to make a border on your February bulletin board. As your students complete the arts and crafts projects on pages 48-56, display their work on this board.

ARTISTS AT WORK

February

• SPONGE AND TEMPERA BORDER FEBRUARY

Stencil Heart Designs

Materials
red, white and pink construction paper
construction paper, any color
small pieces of sponge
red, white, pink and purple tempera paint
scissors
newspaper

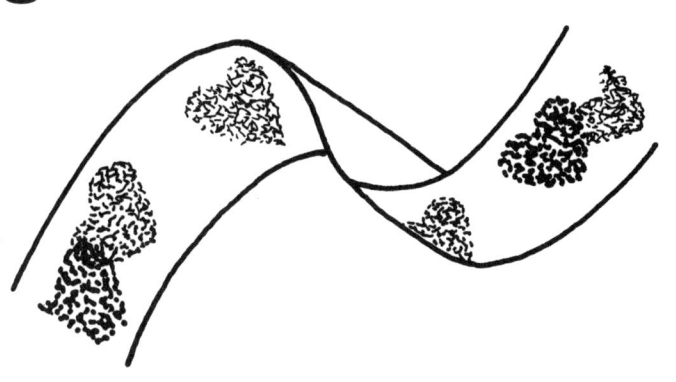

Teacher Preparation
1. Cut red, white and pink construction paper into 4" wide strips. Cut enough to fit around a bulletin board.
2. Cut the remaining construction paper into 3" squares.
3. Cover the art center table with newspaper.
4. Set out the rest of the materials at the art center.
5. Assign students time at the center. Also assign them a certain length of strip to decorate.

Student Directions
1. Fold the construction paper square in half and cut out a heart on the fold as shown. This is your heart stencil.
2. Place the heart stencil over the border strip. Then, dip a sponge into a contrasting color of paint and blot gently over the heart shape with a sponge.
3. Lift your stencil carefully. Then, place the stencil on another part of your border strip and make a sponge design several more times.

Arts and Crafts all through the Year IF8561 © MCMLXXXVIII Instructional Fair, Inc.

• YARN BEAR   FEBRUARY

Fuzzy Bear

Materials
pattern on page 49
9" x 12" brown construction paper,
  one sheet per student
heavy brown yarn
red yarn
scissors
glue
tagboard, one sheet per student
red construction paper (optional)
newspaper

Teacher Preparation
Reproduce one bear pattern on brown construction paper per student.

Student Directions
1. Cover your desk with newspaper.
2. Cut out your bear shape following the outside line.
3. Glue brown bear shape to tagboard and cut out.
4. Cut brown yarn pieces about 1/2" long.
5. Pull the strands of yarn apart.
6. With finger or brush spread glue onto bear body and press yarn into glue. Do a small area at a time until bear is covered with yarn.
7. Tie red yarn around the bear's neck.
8. Cut out a large red heart and glue your bear on top of the heart (optional).

Arts and Crafts all through the Year IF8561   © MCMLXXXVIII Instructional Fair, Inc.

• YARN BEAR　　　　　　　　　　　　　　　　　　　FEBRUARY

Fuzzy Bear Pattern

Arts and Crafts all through the Year IF8561　　49　　© MCMLXXXVIII Instructional Fair, Inc.

•• CHALK AND GLUE HEARTS　　　　　　　　　　　　　　FEBRUARY

Valentine Designs

Materials
9" x 12" white construction paper, one sheet per student
white glue in squeeze bottles
red, pink and purple colored chalk
tissues or cotton
pencils
hairspray or fixative (optional)

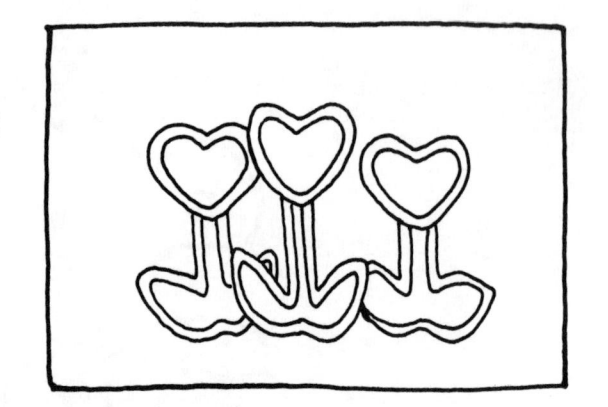

Student Directions
1. Lightly sketch a heart design on white paper with a pencil.
2. Trace the pencil design with thick lines of white glue. Let your design dry completely.
3. Using the side of a piece of red or pink chalk, color the entire heart design.
4. Use your finger, a tissue or cotton to smudge the chalk.
5. Spray the heart design with hairspray or fixative (optional).

Arts and Crafts all through the Year IF8561　　　© MCMLXXXVIII Instructional Fair, Inc.

• PENCIL CARTOONING   FEBRUARY

I Can Draw—Part 1

Materials
drawing paper
pencils

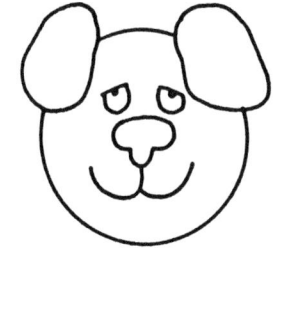

Teacher Directions
1. On the chalkboard draw each pig face, one at a time.
2. After each step, allow the students time to copy your drawing.
3. After you have completed all of the pig's expressions, draw the dog and cat faces on the board so the students can apply the expressions to those animals.
4. After the students complete the dog and cat, have them exchange papers and see if they can guess which expression is shown.
5. Have students write a caption under each expression, such as "I'm feeling low today," or "Yeek, I swallowed a fly," etc.

"Too much ice cream."	"Do you have to leave?"	"Yeek, I swallowed a fly"
"He makes me so mad."	"I'm not telling my secret."	"What a great day!"

Arts and Crafts all through the Year IF8561   51   © MCMLXXXVIII Instructional Fair, Inc.

• CONSTRUCTION PAPER PRESIDENT   FEBRUARY

Mr. Lincoln

Materials
Lincoln pattern on page 53
12" x 18" black construction paper, one sheet per student
oaktag, one sheet per student
white construction paper
crayons
glue
scissors

Teacher Preparation
1. Reproduce the Lincoln pattern onto oaktag.
2. Cut out the pattern and use it for students to trace.
3. Cut out face shapes on white construction paper as shown, or instruct students to cut them out.

Student Directions
1. Trace the Lincoln shape onto black construction paper. Be sure to extend Lincoln's hat so that it is taller than the pattern.
2. Cut out the Lincoln shape.
3. Cut out a face from white construction paper and draw in eyes, nose and mouth. Glue face onto black shape.
4. If you want to fold up your Lincoln shape, see instructions below.

How to Fold

Arts and Crafts all through the Year IF8561

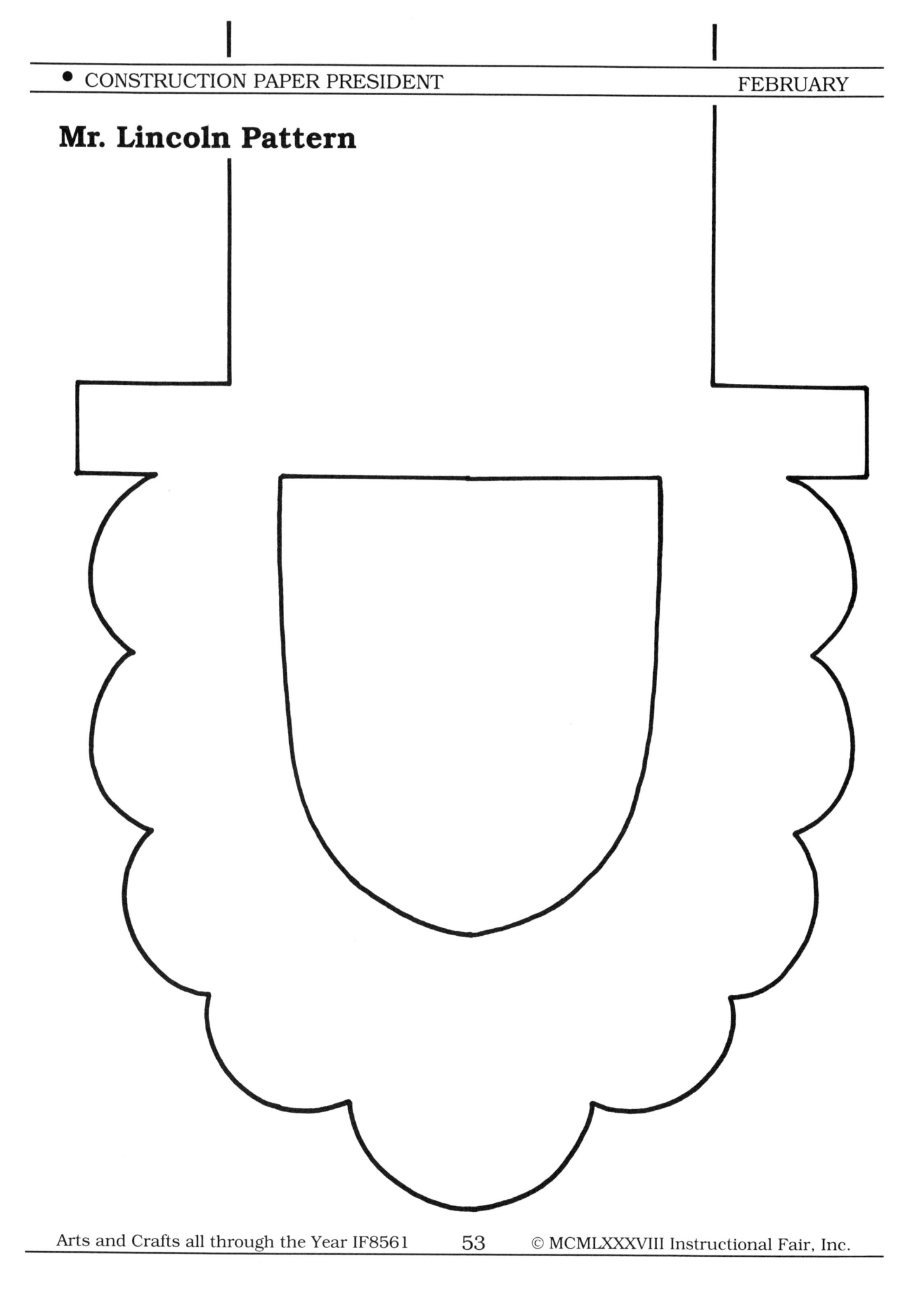

• CONSTRUCTION PAPER PRESIDENT   FEBRUARY

Mr. Lincoln Pattern

Arts and Crafts all through the Year IF8561   53   © MCMLXXXVIII Instructional Fair, Inc.

• CONSTRUCTION PAPER HAT　　　　　　　　　　FEBRUARY

George Washington's Hat

Materials
hat pattern on page 55
9" x 12" red, white, and blue construction paper,
  one of each color per student
crayons
stapler
glue

Teacher Preparation
Using the hat pattern, reproduce three hat pieces per student: one on red, one on white and one on blue construction paper.

Student Directions
1. Cut out the three hat pieces.
2. Staple the pieces together at the corners.
3. Using construction paper scraps or crayons, decorate your hat with stars and stripes.

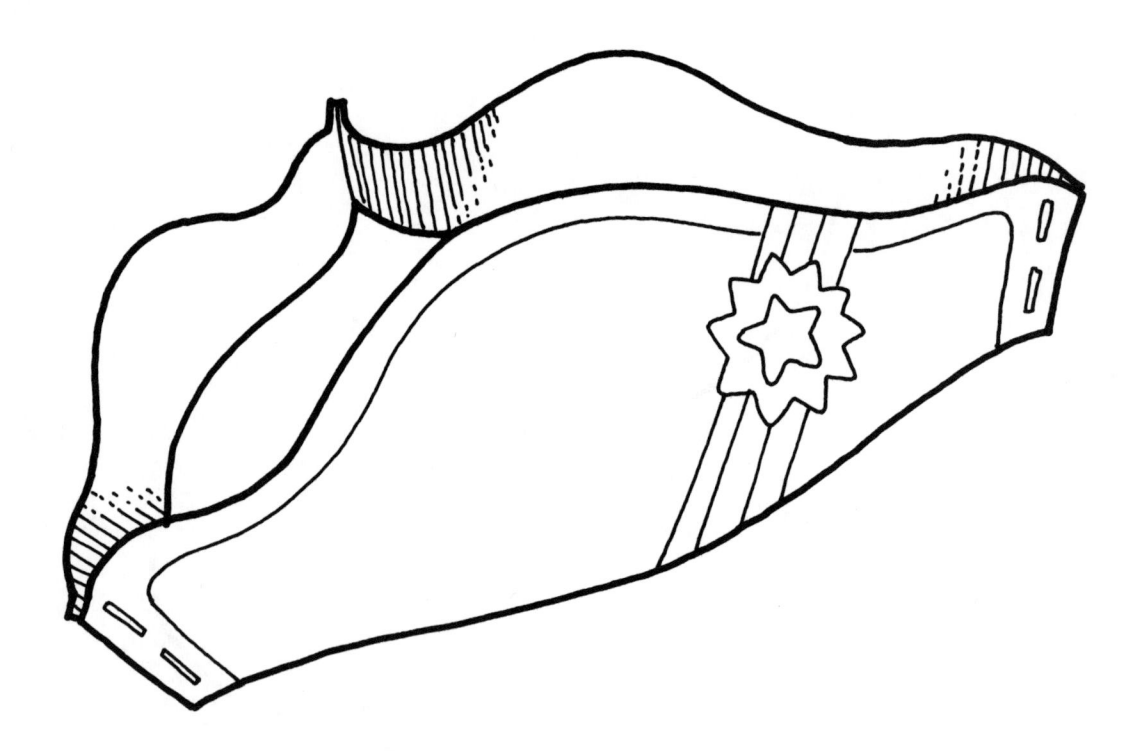

Arts and Crafts all through the Year IF8561　　© MCMLXXXVIII Instructional Fair, Inc.

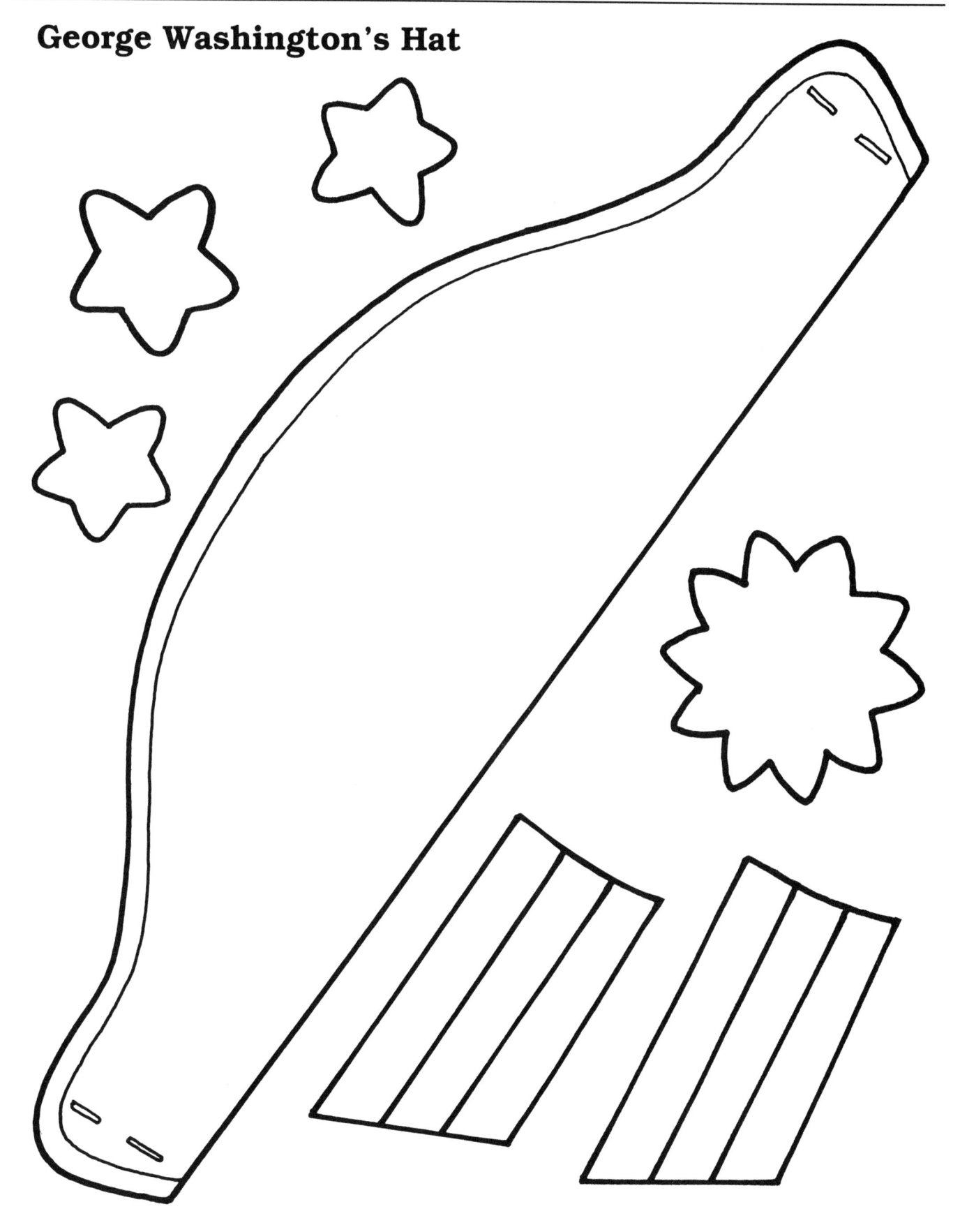

• CONSTRUCTION PAPER HAT   FEBRUARY

George Washington's Hat

Arts and Crafts all through the Year IF8561   55   © MCMLXXXVIII Instructional Fair, Inc.

BALLOON, YARN AND GLUE DESIGNS FEBRUARY

Yarn Balloon Art

Materials
assorted colors of yarn
balloons, one per child
liquid starch
dishes
newspaper

Teacher Preparation
Cut about 20 pieces of 20" yarn for each student. Each student should have assorted colors.

Student Directions
1. Cover your desk with newspaper.
2. Blow up your balloon and tie the end in a knot.
3. Dip a piece of yarn into the bowl of starch. Then wrap the yarn around your balloon.
4. Dip and wrap until you have used up all of your yarn.
5. Let the yarn dry.
6. Pop your balloon.

Finishing Touches.
Yarn designs can be hung from the ceiling with a piece of yarn or string.

Variation
Use red, white and pink for a Valentine's party.

MARCH BULLETIN BOARD

Have your students make the shamrock on page 58. Use the shamrocks to make borders on your March bulletin board. The students may need to make several shamrocks each, depending on the size of your bulletin board. As your students complete the arts and crafts projects on pages 59-64, display their work on this board.

Arts and Crafts all through the Year IF8561

• **CONSTRUCTION PAPER BORDER** MARCH

Cartoon Shamrocks

Materials
shamrock pattern below
green construction paper
construction paper scraps, assorted colors
glue
crayons or markers

Teacher Preparation
Duplicate the shamrock pattern on green construction paper.

Student Directions
1. Cut out the shamrock.
2. Draw a face on the shamrock. Be sure to show a definite expression (happy, sad, confused, etc.) as you did in the first cartooning lesson with pigs, dogs and cats.
3. Make a hat from construction paper and glue it to your shamrock.

Arts and Crafts all through the Year IF8561   © MCMLXXXVIII Instructional Fair, Inc.

• TEMPERA PAINTING   MARCH

Blob-Painted Kites

Materials
white construction paper, one sheet per student
tempera paint, all bright colors
paint brushes
crayons or markers
yarn
tissue paper scraps
newspaper

Teacher Preparation
Cut white construction paper into 9" squares.

Student Directions
1. Cover your desk with newspaper.
2. Fold your construction paper square in half, diagonally.
3. Paint or drop blobs of different-colored thick paint on one side of the paper.
4. Refold the paper down the center.
5. Press the paper together and unfold.
6. Let your blob painting dry.
7. Use crayons or markers to draw a border around your kite.
8. Use yarn to add a tail to your kite.
9. Make bows with tissue paper, as shown. Staple the bows onto the kite tail.

Arts and Crafts all through the Year IF8561

• PAPER CRAFT   MARCH

Jumping O'Jiminy Leprechaun

Materials
leprechaun parts on page 61
9" x 12" white construction paper, one sheet per student
9" x 12" green construction paper
crayons or markers
glue or tape

Teacher Preparation
1. Reproduce leprechaun parts onto white construction paper, one complete leprechaun per student.
2. Cut 1" x 9" strips from green construction paper, four strips per student.

Student Directions
1. Cut out the leprechaun parts. Draw in a face and color the rest of his body and hat.
2. Glue the head to the body and the hat to the head.
3. Accordion fold four strips of green construction paper as shown.
4. Glue these strips to the body to form the leprechaun's legs and arms.
5. Glue hands and feet to your leprechaun.

Variation
To make the leprechaun's arms and legs moveable, attach them with brads instead of glue.

Arts and Crafts all through the Year IF8561   © MCMLXXXVIII Instructional Fair, Inc.

• PAPER CRAFT   MARCH

Jumping O'Jiminy Leprechaun

Arts and Crafts all through the Year IF8561   61   © MCMLXXXVIII Instructional Fair, Inc.

• CRAYON-RESIST WATERCOLOR PAINTING   MARCH

Starry, Starry Night

Materials
oaktag
9" x 12" white construction paper,
  one sheet per student
crayons of different shades of blue
  and purple
dark blue or black watercolor paint
paint brushes
newspaper

Teacher Preparation
Draw and cut out several star shapes from oaktag to use as tracers.

Student Directions
1. Cover your desk with newspaper.
2. Using blue and purple crayons, draw a starry night sky design on white construction paper. Make sure you fill the entire page. Color heavily with crayons. If you wish, use the star shapes as tracers.
3. Use dark blue or black watercolors to paint over the entire design. Paint over your design only one time.

Arts and Crafts all through the Year IF8561   © MCMLXXXVIII Instructional Fair, Inc.

• CRAYON OR MARKER DESIGNS   MARCH

Patterned Shamrocks

Materials
shamrock patterns below
oaktag
drawing paper, one sheet per student
crayons or markers

Teacher Preparation
1. Reproduce one shamrock pattern set below on oaktag for each student.
2. Demonstrate how to overlap shamrocks and illustrate how different patterns inside each one make an interesting design.

Student Directions
1. Using the shamrock pattern, draw overlapping shamrocks.
2. In each shamrock draw and color a different design.

Arts and Crafts all through the Year IF8561   © MCMLXXXVIII Instructional Fair, Inc.

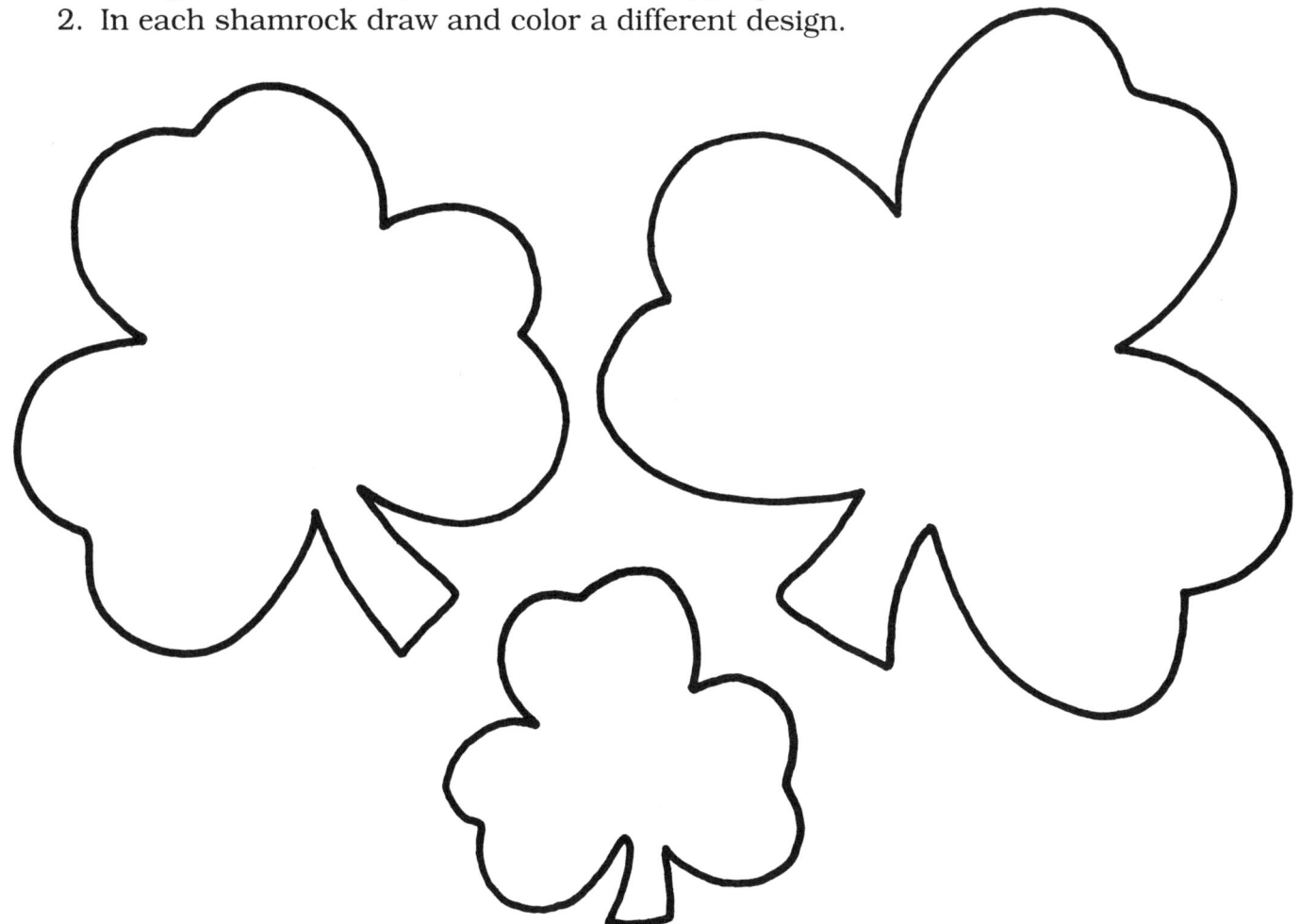

••• TEMPERA PAINTING, GROUP MURAL   MARCH

Fruit and Vegetable Printing

Materials
butcher paper to fit bulletin board
vegetables and fruit pieces that reveal interesting
   patterns when cut in half (apples, oranges, onions, cabbage, etc.)
knife
tempera paint
tin pie plates
newspaper

Teacher Preparation
1. Ask each student to bring in one fruit or vegetable.
2. Cut each fruit or vegetable in half.
3. Pour tempera paint into tin pie plates.
4. Cover floor or large table with newspaper.
5. Place butcher paper on newspaper.
6. Let several students work on printing at a time.

Student Directions
1. Dip your vegetable or fruit half in paint.
2. Stamp the vegetable or fruit half onto the paper gently. Then lift straight up.
3. Dip and stamp again to create a design.
4. Repeat the procedure experimenting with placing your stamp in different directions and creating overlapping shapes.

Note
This bulletin board can stand alone or can be used as backing for the art bulletin board. Or students can make individual projects.

APRIL BULLETIN BOARD

Have your students make the bugs on page 66. Use the bugs to make borders on your April bulletin board. The students may need to make several bugs each, depending on the size of your bulletin board. As your students complete the April arts and crafts projects on pages 67-72, display their work on this board.

Arts and Crafts all through the Year IF8561 © MCMLXXXVIII Instructional Fair, Inc.

• CONSTRUCTION PAPER BORDER   APRIL

April Bugs

Materials
bug patterns below
red and black construction paper
scissors
black markers
glue

Teacher Preparation
Duplicate the bugs on red paper.

Student Directions
1. Trace and cut out bug shapes from red paper.
2. Cut out black circles or stripes and glue them to the bug's shell.
3. Add eyes and mouth with construction paper.

Arts and Crafts all through the Year IF8561   © MCMLXXXVIII Instructional Fair, Inc.

••• PAPER TOWEL ROLL CREATION — APRIL

Spring Creature

Materials
paper towel cardboard rolls
colorful paper of all types (tissue paper, wrapping paper, construction paper)
scissors
glue
miscellaneous decorative items such as cotton balls, fabric scraps, yarn, felt, buttons, beans, tin foil and feathers

Teacher Preparation
1. Have students bring in paper towel rolls.
2. Brainstorm with the students about what sort of new creature might appear in the spring. If they were to create a new creature, what would it look like? Would it have eyes, mouth, arms, legs or fur?

Student Directions
1. Imagine what your spring creature will look like.
2. Cover your towel roll with materials or paper, if you wish.
3. Using decorative items and paper scraps, create a creature. Add your creature's legs, eyes, antennae, toenails—whatever features it might possess.

••• MOSAIC DESIGN   APRIL

Egg Shell Mosaic

Materials
dyed eggshells from Easter eggs
tagboard
markers
glue
newspaper
food coloring (optional)

Teacher Preparation
1. Before Easter, send a note home asking that the shells from all dyed Easter eggs be saved and brought to school.
2. If more shells are needed, they can be dyed in school using food coloring.
3. Crush shells into small, but not tiny, pieces.

Student Directions
1. Cover your desk with newspaper.
2. Using a marker, draw a simple spring shape on a piece of tagboard: a flower, bunny, butterfly, animal, egg, or an abstract design.
3. Spread glue inside this shape.
4. Sprinkle eggshells onto your glue shape, then shake off the extra shell pieces.
5. Design and color in a background, if you wish.

Variation
Use white eggshells instead of colored ones. Have the students use watercolors to lightly paint the shells, after they have completed their designs.

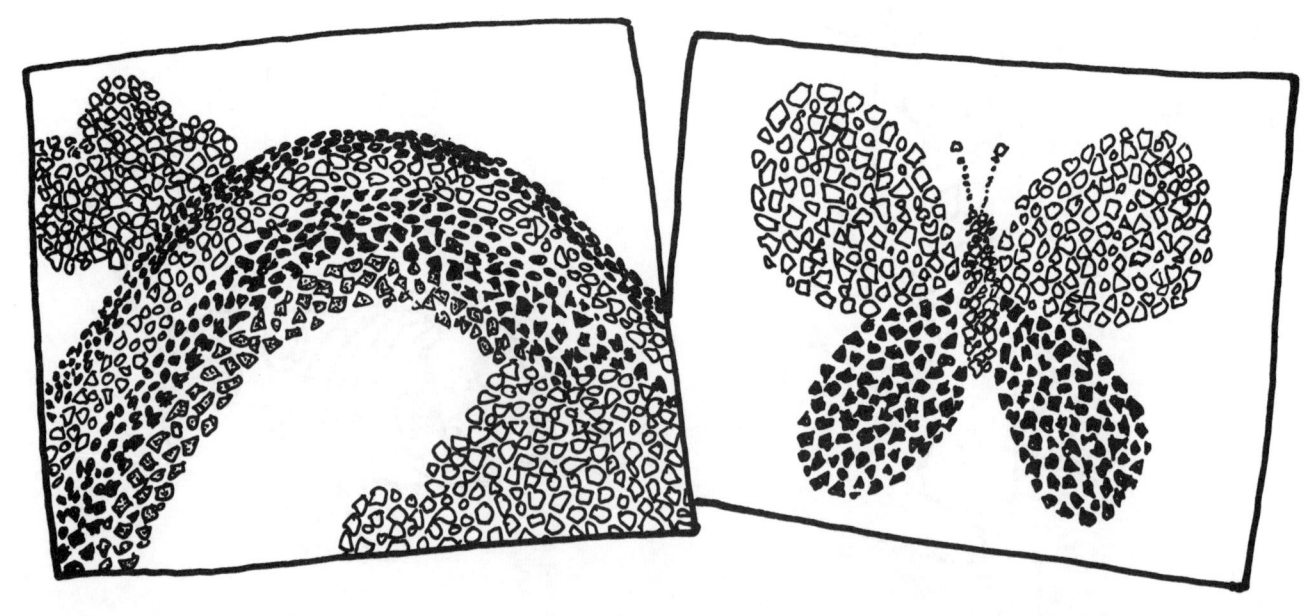

Arts and Crafts all through the Year IF8561   © MCMLXXXVIII Instructional Fair, Inc.

••• FABRIC AND MARKERS, GROUP ACTIVITY   APRIL

Teacher's Skirt or Banner

Materials
white fabric—cotton or muslin, large enough to make a teacher's skirt or banner
permanent felt tipped markers
newspaper

Teacher Preparation
1. Divide the fabric into as many squares as there are students. Be certain to avoid any seam areas which will be sewn together. Use a felt tipped marker to clearly mark the sections.
2. Lay the material out on a table, over newspaper, where several students can work at once.
3. Decide on a theme—spring, school, students' names, etc.

Student Direction
1. At the assigned time pick a square and draw a colorful picture with markers following the class theme.
2. When you are finished, initial your square.

Finishing Touch
Surprise your students by making a skirt from the decorated fabric and wearing it at open house. Parents and students alike will be delighted!

Arts and Crafts all through the Year IF8561   © MCMLXXXVIII Instructional Fair, Inc.

•• MILK CARTON CRAFT   APRIL

Bunny Basket

Materials
bunny parts pattern on page 71
small milk cartons, one per student (see
   variation below if cartons are not available)
9" x 12" construction paper in spring colors
construction paper scraps
tagboard
cotton balls
glue or tape

Teacher Preparation
1. Have the students save milk cartons from lunch. Wash them out and cut them down.
2. Reproduce one set of bunny parts per student on construction paper.
3. Cut out one 1 1/2" x 7" strip of tagboard per student to serve as a handle.
4. Cut out construction paper pieces large enough to cover milk cartons.

Student Directions
1. Wrap a piece of construction paper around your milk carton. Glue or tape the strip in place.
2. Form a face by making a cylinder with the face piece. Add teeth before gluing.
3. Add whiskers and a nose. Glue the face to your carton.
4. Using construction paper, add eyes, ears and other details.
5. Make a tail from a cotton ball.
6. Make a basket handle from the tagboard strip. Glue the handle into place.

Variation
If milk cartons are not available, students can make boxes from construction paper. For a box pattern you can enlarge the one used on page 81. Delete the top of the box pattern.

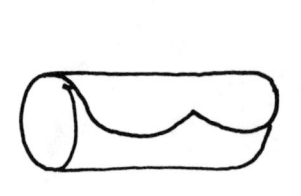

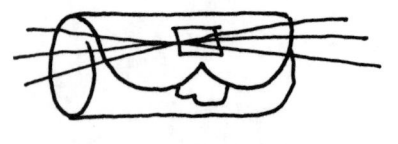

Arts and Crafts all through the Year IF8561   © MCMLXXXVIII Instructional Fair, Inc.

•• MILK CARTON CRAFT   APRIL

Bunny Parts Pattern

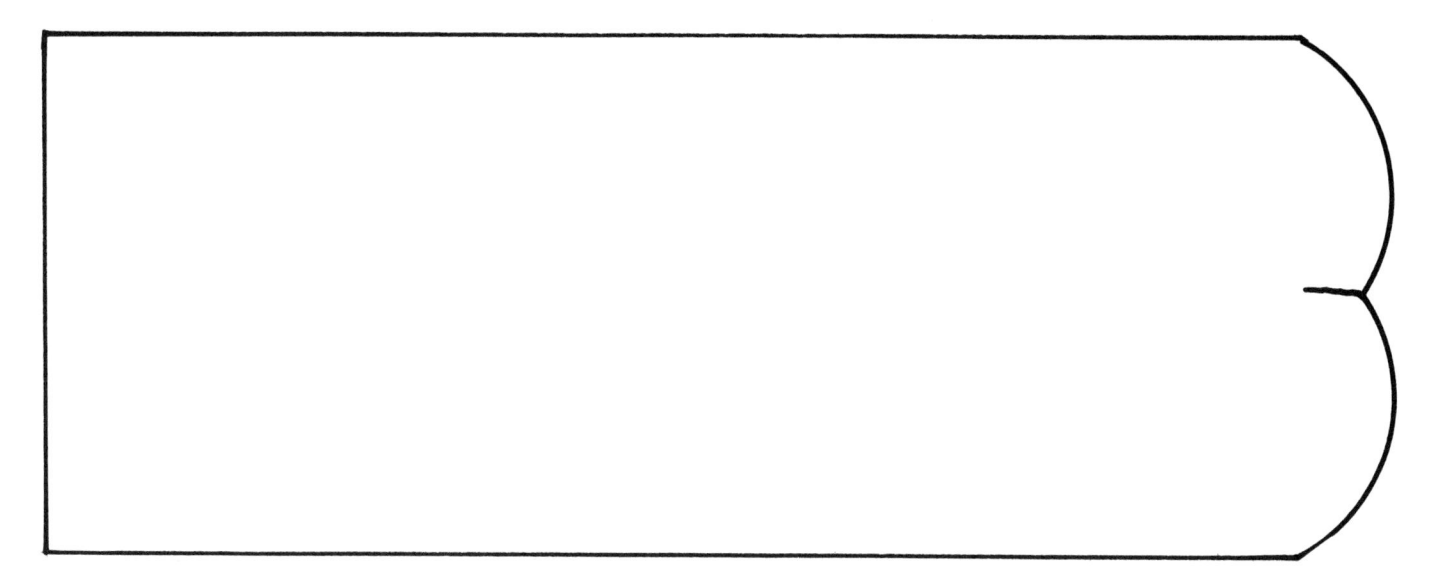

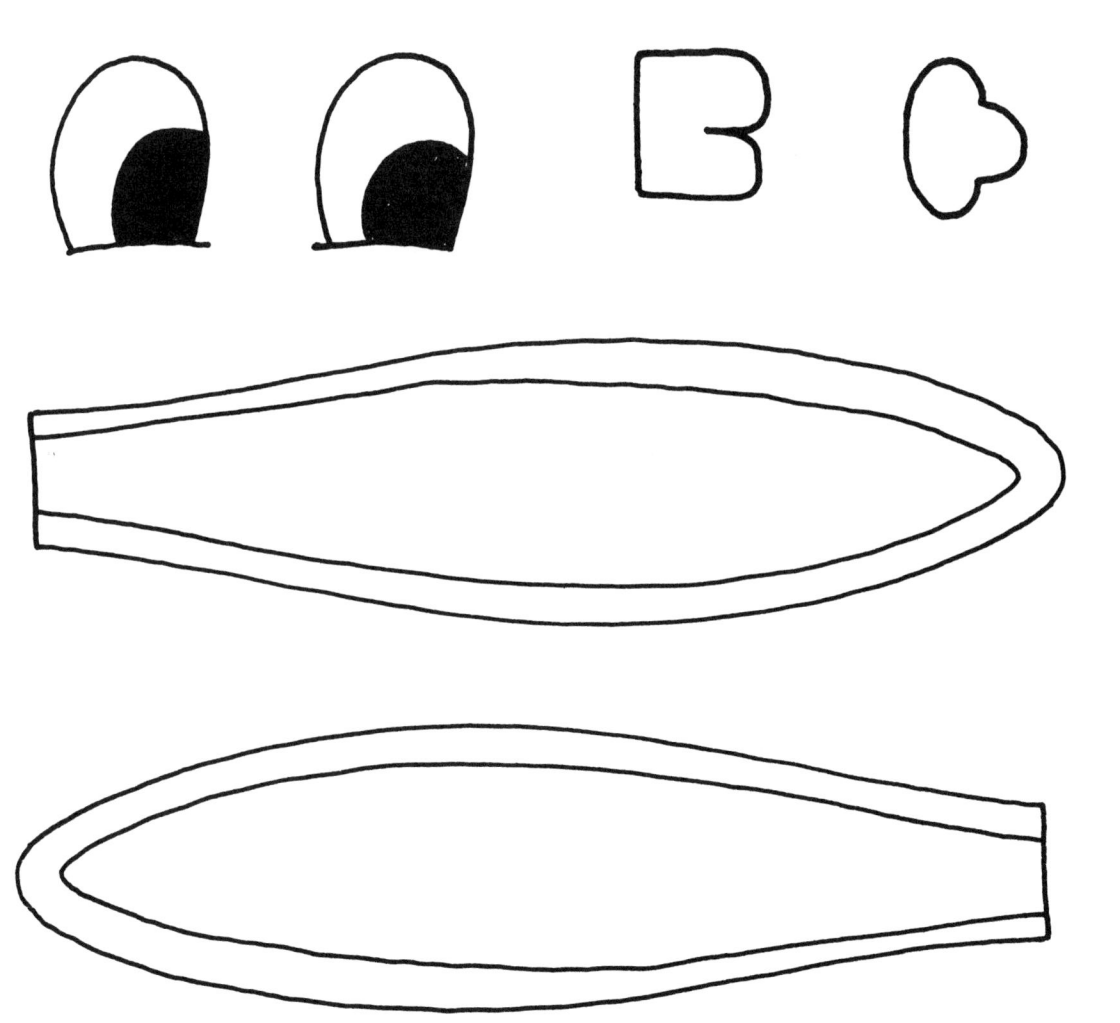

Arts and Crafts all through the Year IF8561   71   © MCMLXXXVIII Instructional Fair, Inc.

•• TEMPERA AND SALT PAINTING   APRIL

Crystallized Egg

Materials
9" x 12" pastel construction paper,
  one sheet per student
tempera paint in bright colors
brushes
pencils
salt
newspaper

Student Directions
1. Cover your desk with newspaper.
2. Draw a simple, large egg with a pencil. Press lightly.
3. Paint your egg using many interesting patterns.
4. While your painting is still wet, sprinkle it with salt.

Variation
Use any easy-to-outline figure (flower, animal, etc.) in place of the egg.

Arts and Crafts all through the Year IF8561

MAY BULLETIN BOARD

Have your students make the flowers on page 74. Use the flowers to make borders on your May bulletin board. The students may need to make several flowers each, depending on the size of your bulletin board. As your students complete the arts and crafts projects on pages 75-81, display their work on this board.

Arts and Crafts all through the Year IF8561 © MCMLXXXVIII Instructional Fair, Inc.

• CONSTRUCTION PAPER BORDER　　　　　　　　　　　　MAY

May Flowers

Materials
construction paper pieces, green and pastel colors
scissors
crayons or markers
glue

Teacher Preparation
1. Cut circles about 1 1/2" in diameter out of construction paper.
2. Cut out 1/2" x 2 1/2" strips of construction paper to make petals.

Student Directions
1. Color a design in the center of the flower.
2. Glue the ends of the petals together as shown.
3. Glue the petals onto the back of the circle as shown.
4. Cut stem and leaves out of green construction paper and glue them to flower.

Arts and Crafts all through the Year IF8561

•• SOAP BUBBLES PAINTING

Bubble Printing

Materials
white construction paper,
  one sheet per student
tempera paint
liquid detergent
water
water container
shallow pans
straws (not flexible), one per student

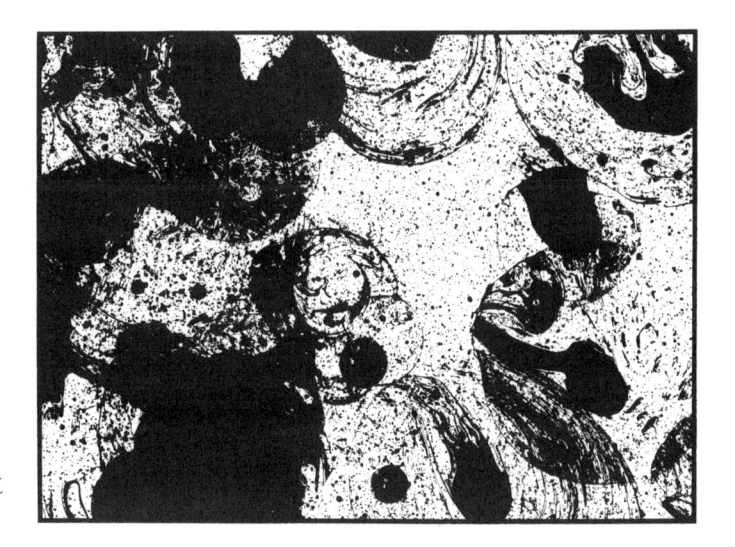

Teacher Preparation
1. Make the following mixture the night before: Mix 1/2 cup tempera paint and 1/2 cup liquid detergent in a quart container. Add water, then stir.
2. Repeat for each color to be used. Let the mixture sit overnight.
3. In class, pour the mixtures into shallow pans.
4. Demonstrate the procedure by blowing into one mixture with a straw to make bubbles.

Student Directions
1. Work in teams of two: a bubble blower and a paper holder.
2. While one student blows bubbles, another student holds his paper 6" over bubbles. When the bubbles break, they will make a design on the paper.
3. Try several colors.
4. Take turns blowing bubbles and holding paper.

Variation
Bring in different types of paper to print on (tissue paper, paper bags).

• TISSUE AND CONSTRUCTION PAPER DECORATIONS   MAY

Stained Glass Butterflies

Materials
12" x 18" black construction paper, one sheet per student
tissue paper in assorted colors
scissors
glue
string (optional)

Student Directions
1. Fold the black paper in half.
2. Draw half an outline of a butterfly. (Younger students repeat the outline 1" inside the first outline as shown. Older students can create more intricate designs as shown.)
3. Cut out the insides of the designs leaving borders as shown.
4. With the design still folded in half, trace the outside shape onto a piece of folded tissue paper and cut out the tissue paper slightly smaller than the construction paper design. (Older students can use different color tissue paper for each section.)
5. Place the black outline frame over the tissue paper and glue them together.
6. Hang the butterfly with string from the ceiling, or place it in the window.

Variation
If you hang your butterfly you might want to back it with another black construction paper frame.

Arts and Crafts all through the Year IF8561   © MCMLXXXVIII Instructional Fair, Inc.

••• MAGAZINE COLLAGE   MAY

Funny Faces

Materials
pictures of faces from magazines
9" x 12" construction paper,
  one sheet per student
glue
scissors

Teacher Preparation
1. Have students bring in pictures of faces from magazines.
2. Cut out, or have students cut out, all parts separately: eyes, ears, nose, mouth and hair.

Student Directions
1. Cut out the parts of the faces. Trade parts with other students.
2. Select parts for your collage: eyes, ears, nose, mouth and hair.
3. Arrange your parts on construction paper to make an interesting or funny face.
4. When you are satisfied with the face, glue down the parts.

•• STENCIL AND SPONGE PAINTING   MAY

Spring Trees

Materials

patterns on page 79
oaktag
dark blue construction paper, one sheet per student
small pieces of brown construction paper
tempera paint in spring colors
sponges
shallow dishes for paint (tin pie plates work well)
masking tape
glue
newspaper

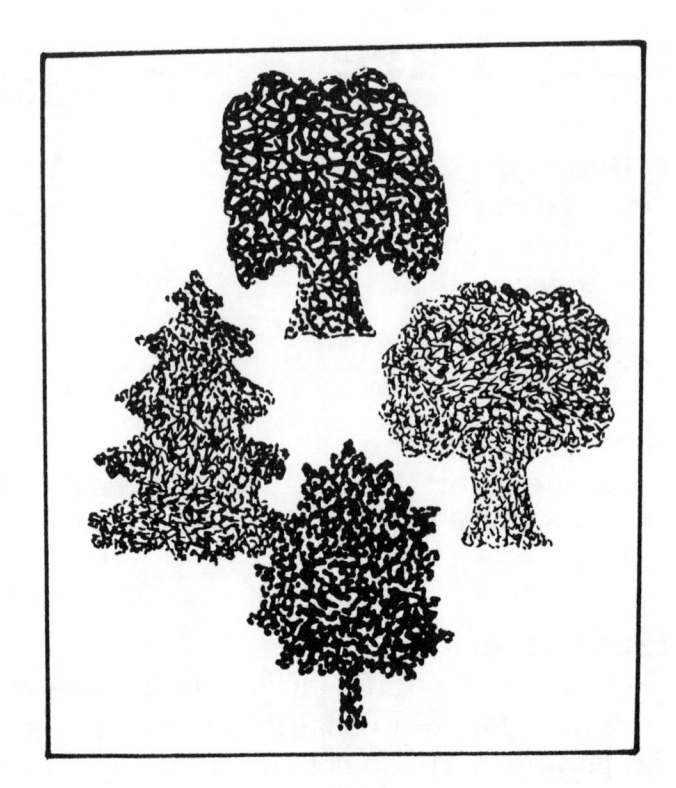

Teacher Preparation
1. Make stencils out of oaktag of different shaped trees using the patterns on page 79. Save the inside of the stencils — they can also be used.
2. Pour paint into shallow dishes, one color per dish.
3. To motivate students for this activity, take them outside. Observe trees: colors, shapes, varieties, flowers, shades of green, blossoming trees, etc. Point out to the students how, when you stand in one place, trees seem to overlap each other.

Student Directions
1. Place your stencil over construction paper, tape or hold it in place, and then dab paint with a sponge inside your stencil onto paper.
2. Repeat this process using different shaped trees. Overlap trees and use different colors.
3. For variety, use the piece from the inside of the stencil, place it on paper, and dab paint around the outside of the shape.
4. Cut out tree trunks from brown construction paper and glue them under the trees.

•• STENCIL AND SPONGE PAINTING   MAY

Spring Tree Patterns

Arts and Crafts all through the Year IF8561   79   © MCMLXXXVIII Instructional Fair, Inc.

• CONSTRUCTION PAPER BOXES MAY

Happy Mother's Day Box

Materials
box pattern on page 81
9" x 12" light construction paper, one sheet per student
white construction paper
crayons or markers
scissors
tape or glue

Teacher Preparation
1. Reproduce copies of box patterns on light construction paper.
2. Cut out message strips from white construction paper, 1 1/2" x 12".

Student Directions
1. Cut out the box pattern on outer solid lines.
2. Color the pictures.
3. Fold in on all small broken lines.
4. Tape or glue the sides of the box together at tabs.
5. Write a Mother's Day message on the strip.
6. Accordion fold the strip.
7. Tape the end of the strip on the inside of the box.
8. Cut slit in top and close.

- CONSTRUCTION PAPER BOXES   MAY

Happy Mother's Day Box

top of box

Happy Mother's Day

slit

Arts and Crafts all through the Year IF8561   81   © MCMLXXXVIII Instructional Fair, Inc.

JUNE BULLETIN BOARD

Have your students make the suns on page 83. Use the suns to make borders on your June bulletin board. The students may need to make several suns each, depending on the size of your bulletin board. As your students complete the arts and crafts projects on pages 84-89, display their work on this board.

ARTISTS AT WORK

June

• CONSTRUCTION PAPER BORDER   JUNE

June Suns

Materials
pattern below
yellow construction paper
orange construction paper
scissors
glue
crayons or markers

Teacher Preparation
Duplicate one yellow and one orange sun per finished sun.

Student Directions
1. Draw a face on one sun. Then fold its rays forward on dotted lines.
2. Glue your sun face on top of the second sun.

DRIED FOOD COLLAGE — JUNE

Macaroni and Bean Collage

Materials
various shapes of macaroni
beans
dry cereal
pop corn
seeds in shells
markers
pencils
glue
styrofoam meat tray, one per student

Teacher Preparation
Have students bring in styrofoam meat trays.

Student Directions
1. Using a pencil, draw a large, simple flower design on your meat tray.
2. Trace your design using a marker.
3. Fill in the design with an assortment of food items.

• Pencil Cartooning   JUNE

I Can Draw—Part 2

Materials
drawing paper
pencils

Teacher Directions
1. On the chalkboard, draw each step shown below, one step at a time.
2. After each step, allow the students time to copy your drawing.

1

2

3

4

5

6

7

Arts and Crafts all through the Year IF8561   85   © MCMLXXXVIII Instructional Fair, Inc.

••• GRASS-IN-A-CUP CRAFT   JUNE

Happy Father's Day Planter

Materials
face parts on page 87
white styrofoam drinking cups, large size,
  one per student
9" x 12" white construction paper,
  one sheet per student
crayons or markers
scissors
glue
potting soil
rye grass seed

Teacher Preparation
Reproduce face parts onto white construction paper, one complete face per student.

Student Directions
1. Carefully fill your cup two-thirds full with potting soil. Sprinkle grass seed on the top of the soil, then cover it with a thin layer of potting soil.
2. Put your cup in a sunny place and water it every few days.
3. The day before you give this plant as a gift, cut out the face parts you would like to use and color them using a crayon or marker.
4. Glue the face parts to the outside of your styrofoam cup.

Note
It will take about seven days for the grass to begin to grow and form the "hair" on the Father's Day gift planter. Make this project two or weeks before Father's Day to allow sufficient time for the grass to grow. Have students glue on the face parts just before giving this plant as a gift. (Once they water the plant they could ruin the face.)

••• GRASS-IN-A-CUP CRAFT   JUNE

Happy Father's Day Planter

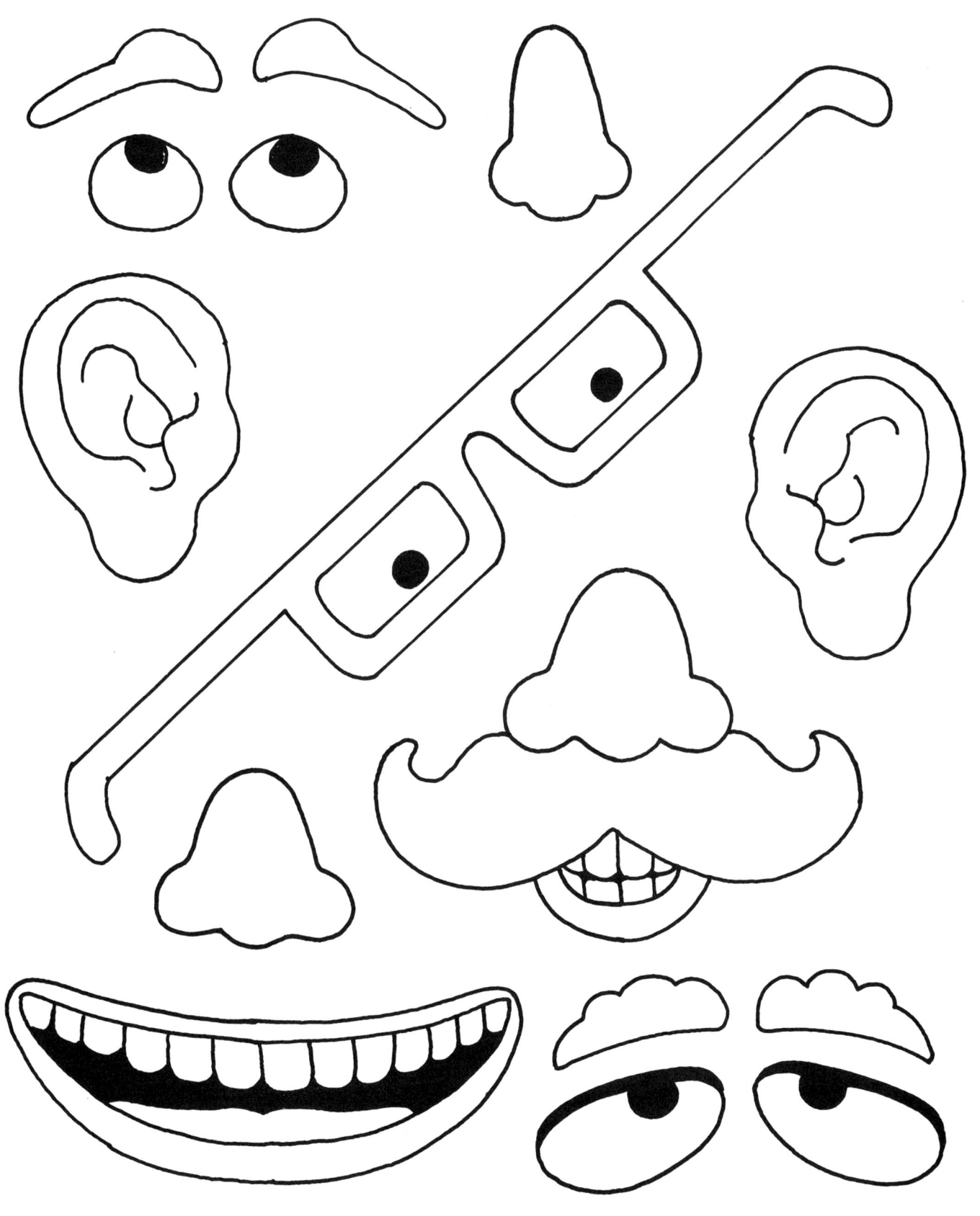

Arts and Crafts all through the Year IF8561   87   © MCMLXXXVIII Instructional Fair, Inc.

•• CRAYON, TEMPERA, AND PLASTIC WRAP PAINTING   JUNE

Underwater Scene

Materials
pictures of underwater scenes
white painting paper,
 one sheet per student
crayons
blue tempera paint
brushes
pencils
plastic wrap
tape
newspaper

Teacher Preparation
1. Dilute the blue tempera to a watery consistency.
2. Show students underwater scenes, and discuss life and objects found underwater: shells, fish, seaweed, etc.

Student Directions
1. Cover your desk with newspaper.
2. Lightly draw an underwater scene with pencil.
3. Color your picture with crayons. Press hard.
4. Brush your entire picture with diluted blue tempera paint.
5. When your picture dries, cover it with plastic wrap. Tape plastic wrap in back.

• PINHOLE DESIGN   JUNE

June Scene

Materials
construction paper
straight pins
pencils
tape

Student Directions
1. Very lightly, draw an outline of a simple shape on your paper.
2. Stick your pin every one-half inch through the outline.
3. Tape your picture to a window and see what happens to the light.

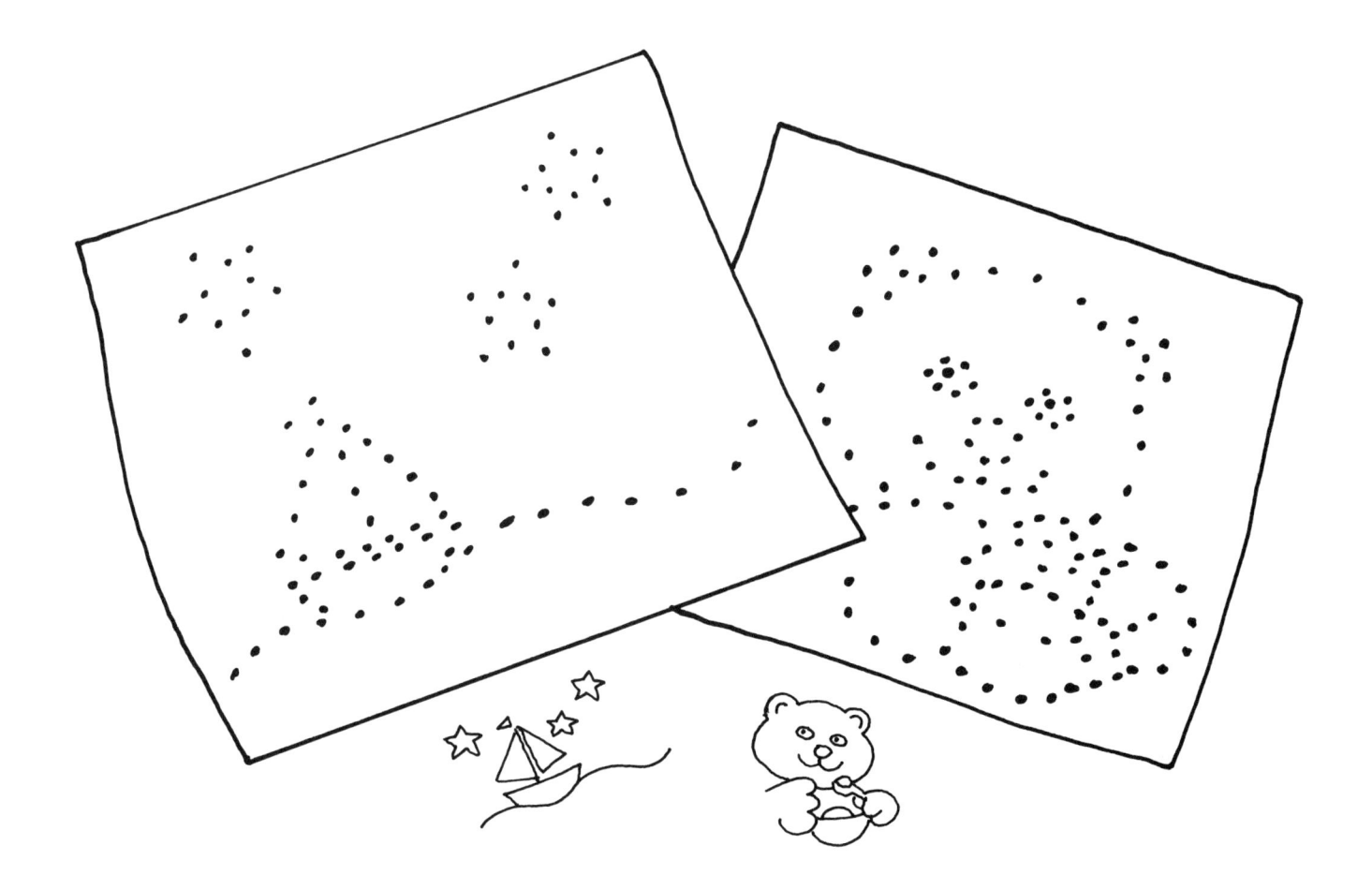

SUMMER BULLETIN BOARD

Have your students make the sailboats on page 91. Use the sailboats to make borders on your summer bulletin board. The students may need to make several sailboats each, depending on the size of your bulletin board. As your students complete the arts and crafts projects on pages 92-96, display their work on this board.

Arts and Crafts all through the Year IF8561 © MCMLXXXVIII Instructional Fair, Inc.

• CONSTRUCTION PAPER BORDER   SUMMER

Summer Sailboats

Material
construction paper
crayons or markers

Teacher Preparation
1. Cut construction paper into 4 1/2" squares.
2. Using the steps below, demonstrate to student how to make a boat.

Student Directions
1. To make a boat, follow your teacher's directions.
2. Decorate your sail with crayons or markers.
3. Name your boat.

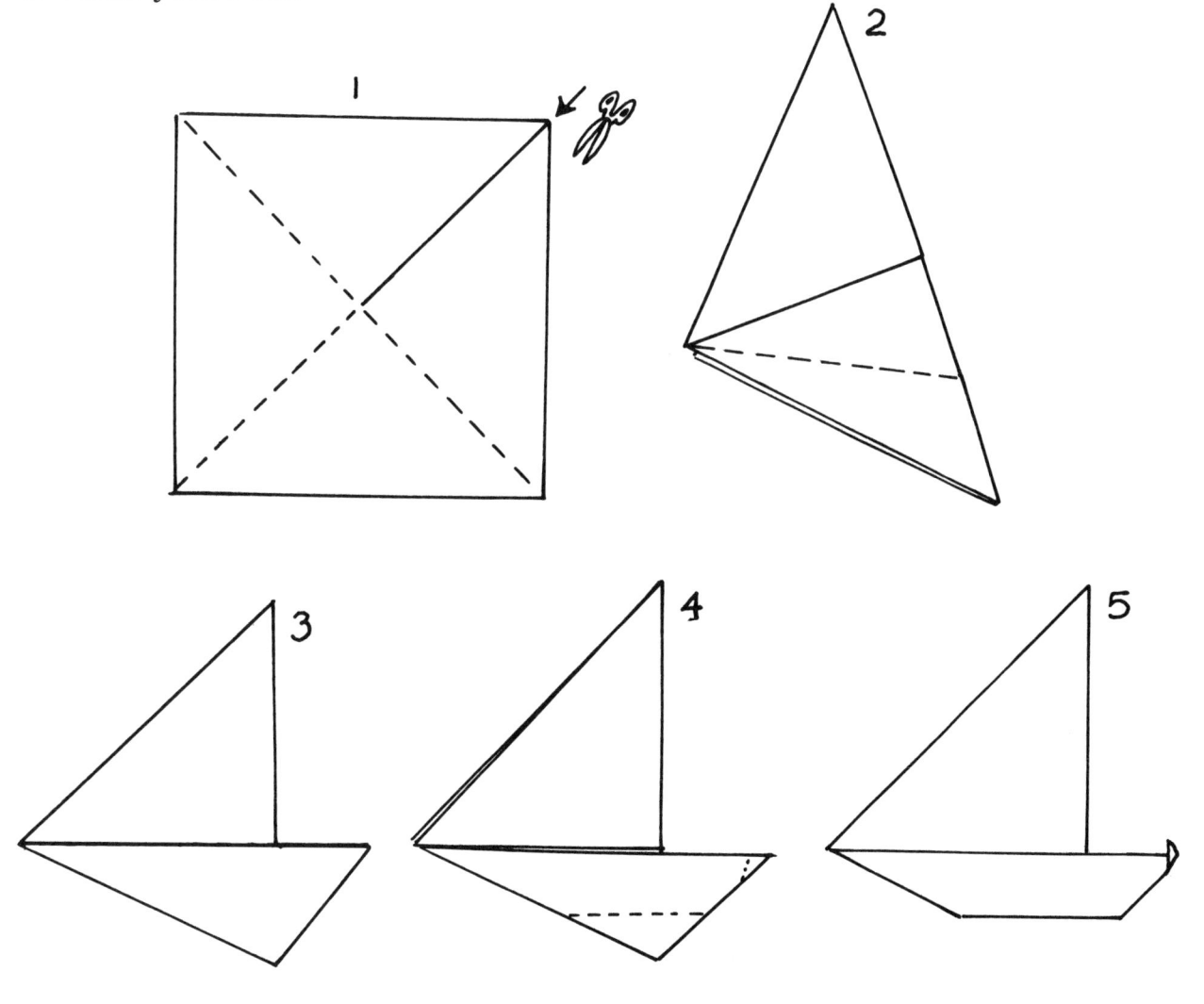

• STRAW BLOW PAINTING   SUMMER

Fourth of July Fireworks

Materials
12" x 18" black construction paper, one sheet per student
light red, white and light blue tempera paint, thinned
containers
drinking straws

Student Directions
1. Begin by putting one large drop at a time of either red, white or blue tempera paint on black construction paper.
2. Using a drinking straw, blow on each paint drop to create a starburst design. Let the paint dry.
3. Choose a different color and repeat the same procedure on a different part of the black paper. Designs will overlap.
4. Repeat the procedure using a third color.

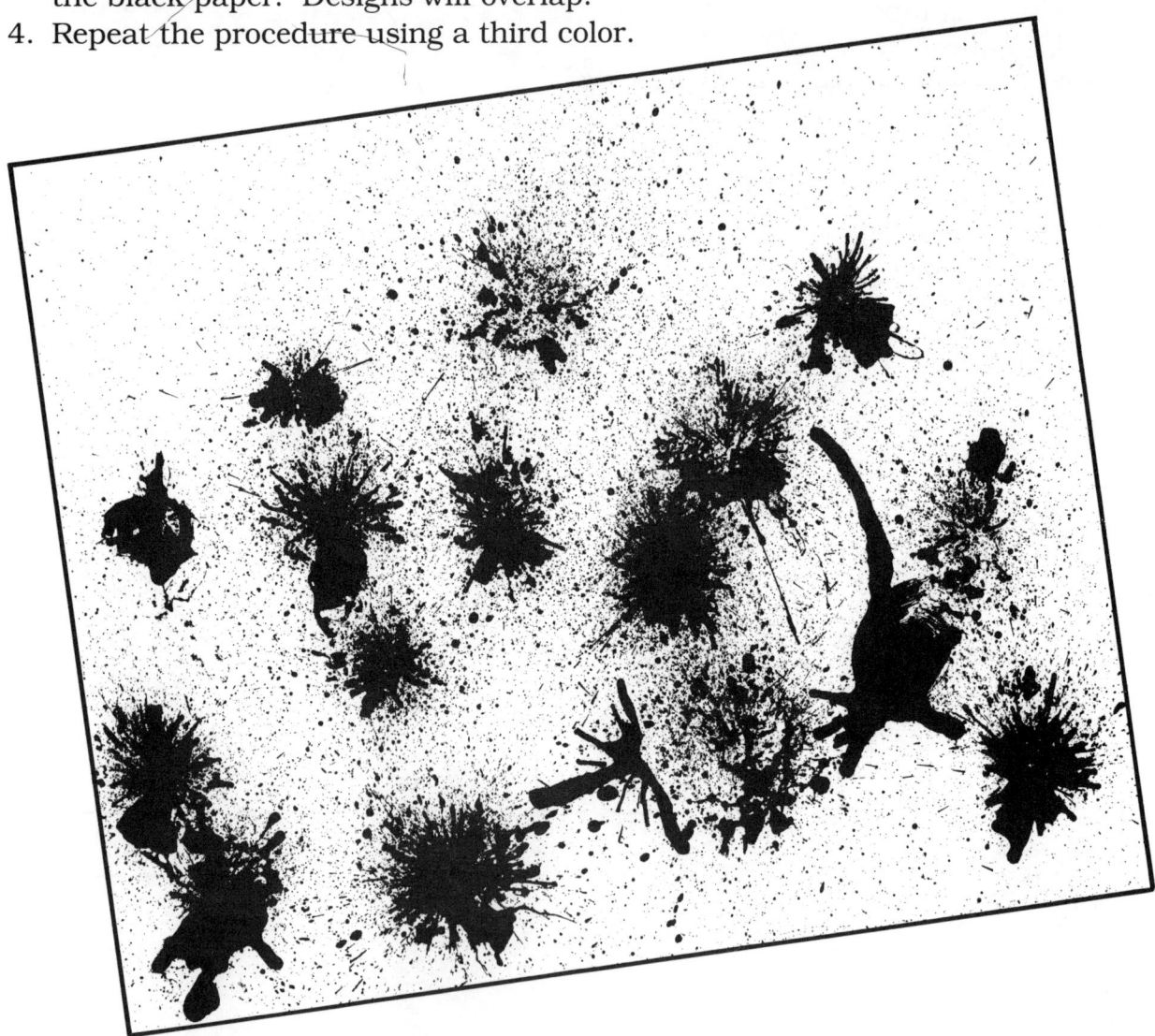

• WATERCOLOR SILHOUETTE DESIGNS   SUMMER

Summer Sunsets

Materials
9" x 12" white construction paper,
   one sheet per student
black construction paper
watercolors
brushes
scissors and glue
masking tape
newspaper

Student Directions
1. Cover your desk with newspaper.
2. Tape a piece of white construction paper onto your desk with masking tape.
3. Wet the entire surface of the white paper using a paintbrush and water. Your paper should be very wet, but it should not have puddles.
4. Using sunset colors such as red and orange, paint one strip at a time across your paper as shown. Because the paper is wet, the colors will run together. Let the paint dry completely.
5. Draw an outdoor scene on black construction paper. Cut out the shapes and glue them to your watercolor.

●● SEWING WITH FELT SUMMER

Felt Hand Puppets

Materials
pattern on page 95
9" x 12" oaktag, one piece per student
felt pieces, two 5" x 7" pieces per student
yarn
thread
pins
needle
glue

Teacher Preparation
1. Reproduce one pattern on oaktag per student.
2. Show students how to thread a needle.

Student Directions
1. Cut out your puppet pattern.
2. Trace the puppet pattern on two different pieces of felt, then cut out the pieces.
2. Place hair on the bottom piece.
3. Pin the two pieces together and stitch them as shown.
4. Cut out pieces of felt and yarn to make eyes, mouth, nose, etc., and glue these to your puppet.

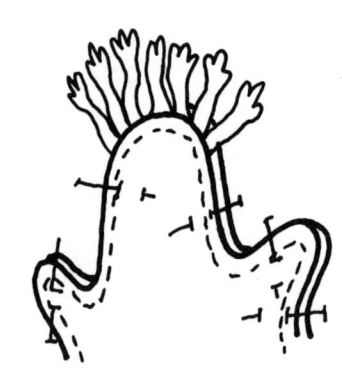

Arts and Crafts all through the Year IF8561

•• SEWING WITH FELT   SUMMER

Felt Hand Puppet Pattern

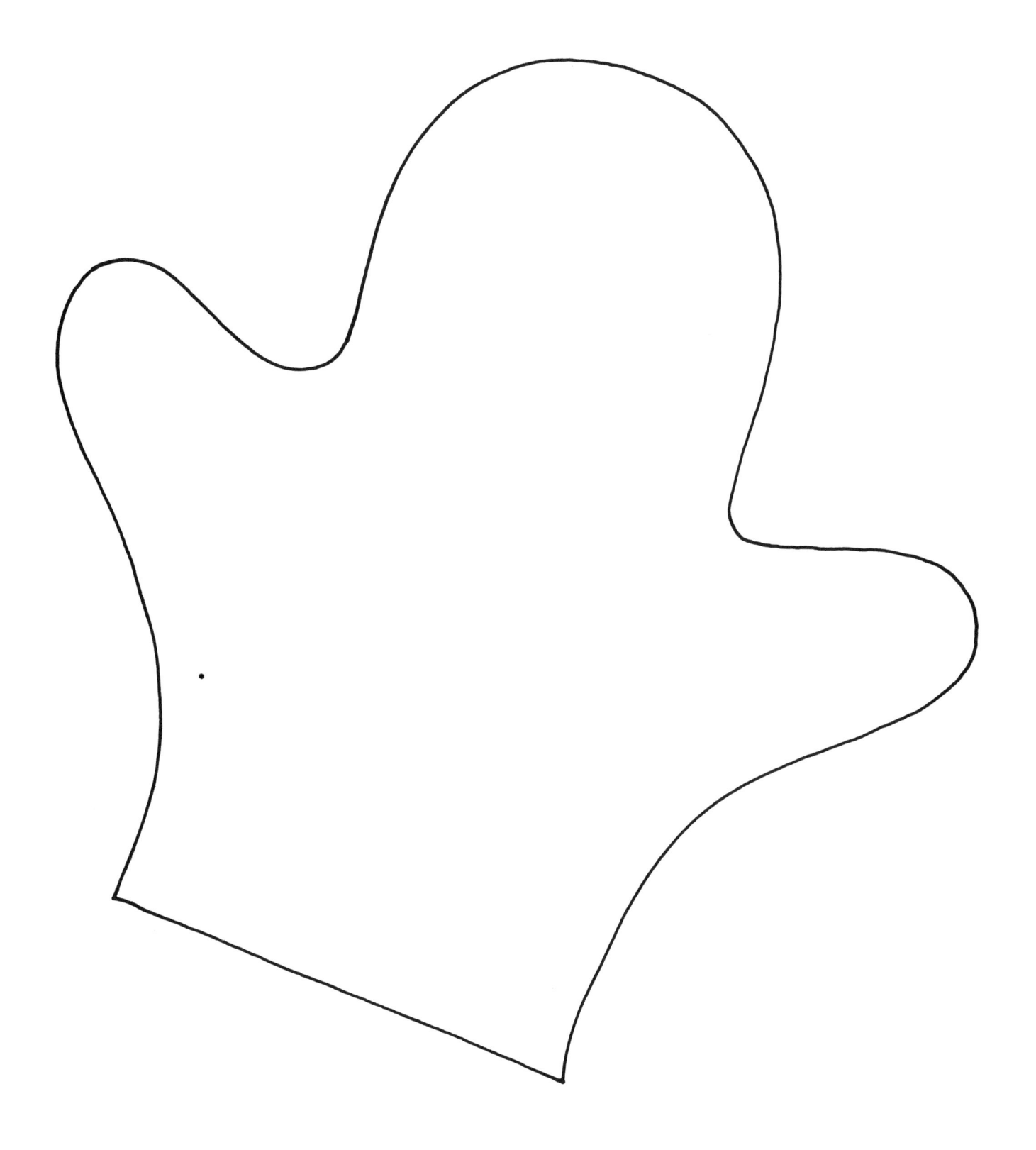

Arts and Crafts all through the Year IF8561   95   © MCMLXXXVIII Instructional Fair, Inc.

• • • TEMPERA PAINTING ACTIVITY   SUMMER

Circle Printing

Materials
construction paper, any color, one sheet per student
construction paper in contrasting color for framing (optional)
tempera paint
any small objects which will print a circle: thread spools,
   glasses, jars, containers, cookie cutters, etc.
newspaper

Teacher Preparation
1. Have students bring in small circular objects.
2. Set out various colors of tempera paint.

Student Directions
1. Dip objects, one at a time, into tempera paint.
2. Press the object onto construction paper, then lift it off, straight up.
3. Experiment with various colors and objects. Try overlapping prints.
4. Back your finished painting with a piece of construction paper (optional).

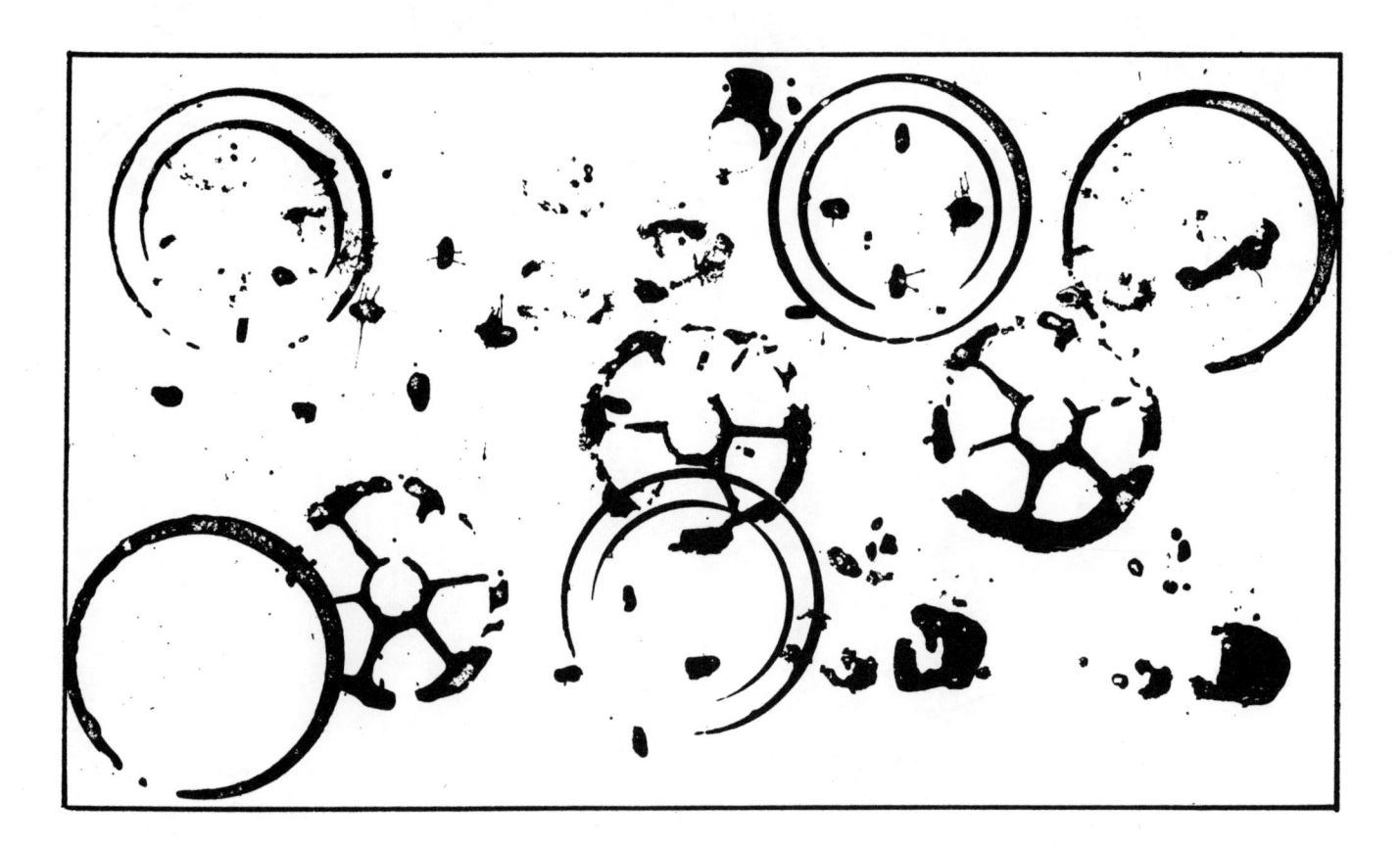